PORTUGUESE
COOKING

AN UNFORGETTABLE JOURNEY
THROUGH THE FLAVOURS AND COLOURS
OF A FASCINATING COUNTRY

HOW TO READ THE CARDS

DIFFICULTY	FLAVOUR	NUTRITIONAL CONTENT
● Easy	● Mild	● Low
●● Medium	●● Medium	●● Medium
●●● Difficult	●●● Strong	●●● High

Preparation and cooking times are shown in hours (h) and minutes (e. g. 30' is 30 minutes).

Most of our recipes, especially those that require a certain amount of attention during their preparation, are illustrated with a series of step-by-step photographs to help the cook. We suggest you read the list of ingredients carefully (as well as the charts, which indicate how long it will take to prepare and cook the dishes, their difficulty, the strength of their flavour, their nutritional value), then every step of the method, all before attempting it. Then, of course – *bon appetit*!

NOTES AND SUGGESTIONS TO READERS:
In the text oven temperatures are given in centigrade. The following conversion chart may be useful:

150 °C/ 300 °F/ GAS MARK 2
160 °C/ 325 °F/ GAS MARK 3
175 °C/ 350 °F/ GAS MARK 4
190 °C/ 375 °F/ GAS MARK 5
200 °C/ 400 °F/ GAS MARK 6
220 °C/ 425 °F/ GAS MARK 7
230 °C/ 450 °F/ GAS MARK 8

Project: Casa Editrice Bonechi
Series editor: Alberto Andreini
Concept and co-ordination: Paolo Piazzesi
Graphic design: Andrea Agnorelli and Maria Rosanna Malagrinò
Cover: Maria Rosanna Malagrinò
Make-up: Rita Bianucci
Editing: Patrizia Chirichigno

Translation: Shona C. Dryburgh

Chef: Lisa Mugnai
Dietician: Dr. John Luke Hili

The photographs illustrating the recipes are property of the Casa Editrice Bonechi *photographic archives and were taken by* Andrea Fantauzzo.

The illustration on the title page was taken by Andrea Fantauzzo *and is the property of the* Casa Editrice Bonechi *archives.*

The photographs of places and scenery are property of the Casa Editrice Bonechi *photographic archives and were taken by* Paolo Giambone *and* Jean Charles Pinheira.

The Publisher is grateful for any information concerning the photographs with no identified author and will be pleased to acknowledge the relative sources in future editions.

© Copyright 2002
by CASA EDITRICE BONECHI, Florence - Italy
E-mail: bonechi@bonechi.it   Websites: www.bonechi.it   www.bonechi.com

Printed in Italy by Centro Stampa Editoriale Bonechi.

ISBN 88-476-0921-6

***

INTRODUCTION

Our journey through the various flavours and colours of Lusitanian cuisine is a tribute to the regions that are renowned for their cooking traditions and famous dishes, but we shall also visit other areas in the country where their kitchens often hide delicious treasures.

Our tour starts in the North-East, at Trás-os-Montes. Here, between woody hills and green fields we find Peso da Régua, the city that sits among the vineyards that produce the grapes for Port: barrels of the

famous wine used to be shipped from here or from Pinhão and sent down the river Douro to the cellars where they were left to mature. Then we come to Vila Real, Murça, Miranda do Douro on the Spanish borders, Bragança, the stronghold still surrounded by walls, and Chaves, famous for its delicious cured ham as well as its spa, which was well known even in Roman times. The food in this area is hearty and satisfying, and from the many enticing dishes we have chosen *caldo de cebola*, *bola de bacalhau*, *coelho de cebolada*, and the famous *cozido à portuguesa* with *chicharros*.

Oporto, the second largest city in Portugal and the place where the aromatic wine bearing the same name matures in splendid cellars, sits on the estuary of the river Douro. From the traditional fare of the Douro area we have selected *santola no carro*, an exquisite hors-d'œuvre, then *arroz de bacalhau* and *bacalhau à Gomes de Sá*, finishing with *aletria com ovos* and the celebrated *toucinho do céu*. Going North, towards the river Minho, we come across Vila do Conde, Barcelos, Baroque Braga, mediaeval Guimarães and picturesque Amarante. Here, besides delicious dishes prepared with dried codfish, like *bacalhau à lagareiro* and *bacalhau podre*, we can enjoy *truta à moda de Barroso* served with *tomatada com batatas*.

In the region called after the river Minho, which runs along the Spanish border, we meet Viana do Castelo, a fishing and tourist port, Ponte da Barca, and the ancient strongholds of Arcos de Valdevez and Monção. This is the area that produces outstanding salamis and cured meats, as well as what is called *vinho verde* – a light, sparkling red or white wine named 'verde' because this means 'young' – and nobody should leave here without having tasted *caldo verde*, a cabbage and potato soup that has become a national dish, or *rancho à moda do Minho*, or even *pastéis de bacalhau*, *rojões com belouras*, and ending the meal with *arroz doce*.

In the southern part of the Douro region lie the two Beira areas, linked by the same name but each with distinctly different scenery. In Beira-Alta (upper Beira), a land of castles, we find Viseu, famous for its art, and then Guarda, the highest city above sea level in Portugal, at the foot of the Serra da Estrela. Besides the various hams, cheeses, exquisite *morcelas* (see the Explanations on page 6) and extremely palatable wines, we can dine here on *arroz de cabidela* or *sopa de Beira*, *bacalhau assado com batatas a murro* and *trutas abafadas*, or perhaps *vitela assada* cooked in a crust of coarse salt with *batatas de caçoila* or *esparregado de feijão verde*.

Chestnut woods, wheat fields, market gardens, and vineyards that produce the noble Mação wine: this is Beira-Baixa, the heart of Portugal where Castelo Branco, Fundão, Penamacor, the Winter-sports resort called Covilhã, and Belmonte with its castle can be found among rugged slopes and gently rolling hills. The fine dishes made here offer us *pastéis de molho*, *bacalhau à Assis*, *abóbora* and *beringelas fritas*, or the delicious *tigelada*, a golden, oven-baked custard.

Then at last we come to Beira-Litoral (coastal Beira), the land of magical Coimbra, famous for its churches, fountains and the ancient university, near the ruins of Roman Conímbriga; of Aveiro, with its lagoon and salt-pits; of Lousã and Figueira da Foz. Here, the scenery is as varied as the fish dishes are, delicacies that are enhanced further by the fine local wines: after starting with *mexilhões à moda de Aveiro*, an appetising hors-d'œuvre of skewered mussels, we suggest a plate of *arroz de polvo* or hearty *migas da Lousã*, followed by *bacalhau assado com broa* (bread made with maize flour), *caldeirada de enguias* or *raia com molho de pitau*. As cake or dessert we can choose from *broinhas de Natal, charcada, lampreia de ovos* and *queijadas de Coimbra*.

Next stop is the Ribatejo area, on the left banks of the river Tagus, where weeping willows reflect in ponds and rice-fields: this is where we can admire the Gothic churches and towers at Santarém, the Visigoth Santa Irmé; the Manuel-period doorway of the church called Igreja Matriz di Golegã; then whitewashed Abrantes, full of flowers and near Tomar, the city of the Templars with its Convento de Cristo. Sipping the fragrant Cartaxo, Almeirim and Chamusca wines, we can enjoy *migas de pão de milho* or the traditional *sopa de pedra*, then *fataça na telha* or *cabrito assado* accompanied by *batatas de rebolão*, and to finish, *fios-de-ovos*.

Estremadura holds a real jewel: Lisbon, the westernmost European capital, which lies within an amphitheatre of hills that reflect in the river Tagus and the Atlantic Ocean. Leaving this city, as busy as the Baixa area and as melancholic as the *fado*, welcoming yet engrossed with its own life, we then head for

Looking down on Santarém.
On the previous page: part of the port at Lagos, Algarve.

Costa da Prata, passing Estoril and Cascais. Here we find Moorish influence in Sintra, with its beautiful gardens, Mafra with its immense convent-palace, historical Torres Vedras and Peniche, the ancient town of Óbidos, the old sulfur springs at Caldas da Rainha, Nazaré with its beaches, Alcobaça and its convent and the monastery at Batalha, a Gothic masterpiece. Leiria appears, with its castle and enormous pine woods, then Marinha Grande with Fátima nearby. The food in this area is outstanding, starting from the hors-d'œuvre: *amêijoas à Bulhão Pato, ovos verdes, pataniscas de bacalhau, peixinhos da horta*; next, we can choose from *açorda de camarão* and *sopa rica de peixe*, followed by *bacalhau à Brás* or a fine *lagosta à moda de Peniche, pargo no forno* and *sardinhas assadas*. For meat-lovers there is *bifes de cebolada* and *coelho à caçadora, frango na púcara*, or the traditional *iscas com elas*, slices of liver with potatoes. And why not some *feijoada à portuguesa*, a dish with cured meats swimming in flavoured beans? A meal made from a selection of these dishes must rightly end with *cavacas das Caldas da Rainha*, or *folar da Páscoa o pastéis de nata*.

Next, we come to the enormous Alentejo plateau, between Ribatejo and Algarve, where noble cities lie among wheat fields and cork-oaks; cities like Elvas, in Upper Alentejo, famous for its olives and fortified strongholds, or Estremoz, with its ancient castle, then Redondo, Évora, where the XIII century Sé is both church and fortress. In Lower Alentejo we find Sines, Santiago do Cacém, Grândola and Setúbal, the large port on the Sado estuary, with its splendid Manuel-Gothic Igreja de Jesus. Alentejo cooking is nutritious and very tasty, and Borba, Vidigueira or Reguengos wines enhance the flavours: we can start here with the famous *açorda à alentejana* and *migas à alentejana*, or *sopa da cação*, for those who enjoy fish; next, *empadas de galinha*, followed by *lombo de porco com amêijoas*, loin of pork with clams, or *feijão verde à alentejana*. Lastly, sweet temptations like *bolo-podre* and *pão-de-ló de amêndoas*.

Reaching the extreme South of the country, we come to the Algarve region, which takes its name from the Arab *al gharb* and means 'Western garden'. The Atlantic Ocean washes the shores on two sides of this region, and the landscape is a series of high cliffs, inlets and flat islands with white, sandy beaches: here we see Vila do Bispo, the fortress at Sagres, lively Lagos and Portimão (the Roman Portus Magnus); then Albufeira, perched high on the cliffs, Faro with its the walls and Cathedral, Moorish Olhão, the isle of Tavira and its beaches – and Vila Real de Santo António, on the borders with Spain. The landscape is reminiscent of nearby Africa. The food here is excellent and, of course, fish plays the leading rôle; the sweets are also exceptional, with the famous *morgado*, marzipan made into every shape imaginable, taking pride of place. For a menu we could start with *amêijoas na cataplana*, clams cooked in the special, copper *cataplana* pot with a double, domed lid, *cenouras em conserva* and *choquinhos fritos com tinta*; followed by *arroz de berbigão* or *canja de conquilhas, sopa de feijão-manteiga* or *sopa de langueirão*. Then we could go on to fish dishes, like *atum com tomate*, or the ever-present *caldeirada* or *lulas recheadas*. For those who prefer meat there is a vast selection: *galinha cerejada* or *perna de borrego no tacho* with *ervilhas à moda do Algarve or favas à algarvia*. And the meal could end in glory with *figos recheados*, the famous Algarve figs stuffed with the equally famous Algarve almonds.

Enchanted Madeira awaits us in the Atlantic Ocean: the island of flowers, with Funchal bay and its multi-hued markets. The climate on this island is ideal, to the extent that flora from both temperate and tropical areas, such as orchids, bananas, pineapples – and even sugar canes, thrive here. This is where the cherished Madeira wine is produced in golden vineyards. Fish is abundant and prevalent at the Madeira table: after an appetising *cebolinhas de escabeche* and *sopa de trigo*, we can enjoy *cavalas com molho de vilão* or *carne em vinha-d'alhos com milho frito*.

Our journey ends at the Azores, a ribbon of emerald isles nestling in the blue Atlantic Ocean: Santa Maria, São Miguel with its Rocas Formigas, Graciosa, Terceira, São Jorge, Faial, Pico, Flores and Corvo. This volcanic archipelago, famous for its anticyclone, once

grounds for whale hunting, now lives off tourism, fishing and agriculture. Though Madeira cuisine is outstanding and extremely varied, we have space here to recommend only *cavalas recheadas* and *polvo guisado* – and, of course, its generous cellars.

The picturesque Ponta de Piedade in the Algarve region. Above: a detail of one of the typical boats on the Ria de Aveiro.

A FEW EXPLANATIONS

In some of the recipes you will find certain Portuguese salamis, cured meats and sausages among the ingredients; we shall describe them here so that if you cannot find the real article you will be able to use something similar. *Chouriço* (which brings to mind the Spanish *chorizo*) is a firm, unsmoked sausage stuffed in pig gut (or substitute), between 2.5 and 4 cm (1 ¼ - 2 inches) in diameter, about 40 cm (16 inches) long and bent into a horse-shoe shape. The stuffing, a mixture of not too finely minced lean and fat pork, is usually salted in brine and seasoned with pepper, garlic and ground pimiento, and occasionally a dash of wine. In some areas the *chouriço* is preserved under oil. The *chouriço de sangue* (also known in some areas as *chouriço mouro* or *morcela*, rather like the Spanish *morcilla*) is a smoked sausage stuffed in pig gut and made of minced fatty pork mixed with pig blood and seasoned with salt, pimiento or caraway seeds; it is usually 3 to 4 cm (1 ½ - 2 inches) thick, from 30 to 50 cm (12 - 20 inches) long and is also horse-shoe in shape. Other smoked sausages are *farinheira* and *salpicão*: the first is yet again horse-shoe in shape, no more than 35 cm (14 inches) long, and the pig gut is filled with a mixture of minced fatty pork, flour, pimiento and other spices; the second, roughly cylindrical in shape, is 3.5 to 4.5 cm (1 ¾ - 2 ¼ inches) thick, 14 to 18 cm (6 ¾ - 7 ½ inches) long, and in this case the pig gut is stuffed with finely minced lean and fat pork and seasoned with salt, pepper, garlic and spices. There are many types of Lusitanian cured meats but one of the most delicious is the *presunto*, a prosciutto-type raw ham made from the hind legs of the pig, salt-cured and matured, often smoked and sometimes covered in pimiento paste. One ingredient which is mentioned often is *piri-piri* and it is not difficult to guess what it means: in fact, this is fresh pimiento, usually the red type, more or less hot and spicy, and its size varies depending upon where it is grown. Whenever 'ground pimiento' is mentioned among the ingredients and in the text of a recipe, this means a seasoning (like the Spanish *pimentón*) made from dried *capsicum annuum* pimientos, bright red, mild or hot in flavour (here the choice depends on personal preference and eating habit). This is translated as *paprika* in English speaking countries, which is incorrect, since Hungarian *paprika* is made from an Indian variety of tiny peppers while the *pimentón* spice is made from a variety brought over from the New World. However, though paprika is different in flavour, colour and gastronomic yield, the mild or hot type can be used as a substitute, as can the ground pimiento sold in shops selling biological products.

A FEW WORDS FROM THE DIETICIAN

Portuguese cooking rightly belongs to the series of healthy eating habits that come under the heading of 'Mediterranean Diet'. This diet has some very beneficial characteristics: first, the carbohydrate content, which supplies 55-60% of the daily intake of calories (mainly in complex carbohydrates or starches, large sugar molecules) and guarantees long-lasting energy. Protein content varies around 15% and mainly comes from white meats and 'blue' fish (the inexpensive type caught in local waters); these animal proteins are high in biological value and in the polyunsaturated fats that help prevent cardiovascular disease. Lipid content (25-30% of the daily calories) is principally oleic acid, the main component of olive oil, a mono-unsaturated fat that is the basis of cooking and seasoning in the Mediterranean diet; together with polyunsaturated fats it is valuable for the prevention of arteriosclerosis, and it also has a high 'smoking point'; that is, the temperature at which the molecular structure of the lipid modifies and becomes dangerous to health. Saturated fats modify at lower temperatures. Fibre content is high (at least 25 g per day) and derives mainly from the vegetables commonly grown in the Mediterranean area; these fibres aid bowel movement, combat cholesterol and prevent tumours. Pimiento and other spices are generously used in Portuguese cooking; spices were used in the past as preservatives, especially in hot countries, but now they are added to enhance flavour and make dishes more appetising. Therefore, from a nutritional point of view, Portuguese cooking can be considered very healthy and deserves full consideration.

INDEX OF RECIPES

The elegant 'barcos moliceiros' that sail down the canals in Aveiro, known as the 'Portuguese Venice'.

MEAT AND POULTRY

VEGETABLES AND PULSES

CAKES AND DESSERTS

A detail of the gardens of what was formerly the Bishop's Palace, Castelo Branco.

HORS-D'ŒUVRE AND APPETISERS

*A selection of petiscos, appetisers
and hors d'œuvres to start each meal
with something special and delicious
from both the sea and the countryside,
accompanied by excellent
white and rosé wines.
The recipes are easy to follow, healthy
and easily digested, and never involve
heavy or complicated sauces.
Simple, hearty and enticing:
just like Portugal and its people.*

1

AMÊIJOAS À BULHÃO PATO

Clams in lemon juice ☞ *Estremadura*

Clams, 800 g; 1 ³/₄ lb
2 cloves of garlic
2 lemons
Fresh coriander
2 slices of toasted farmhouse
  bread (for serving)
Pepper
Olive oil

Serves: 6	
Preparation: 5'	
Cooking: 10'	
Difficulty: ●	
Flavour: ● ●	
Kcal (per serving): 210	
Proteins (per serving): 10	
Fats (per serving): 12	
Nutritional value: ● ● ●	

Peel the cloves of garlic and sauté them in a large frying pan with 2-3 tablespoons of oil; remove them as soon as they become golden and put the drained clams in the pan (see below). Lower the heat under the pan, add a few coriander leaves and allow the shells to open, shaking the pan in a circular motion every now and then. Once the clams have opened (discard those that remain closed), add a dusting of pepper and the juice of one lemon. Serve immediately as a starter, accompanying the dish with the other lemon cut into wedges and fingers of toasted bread. Extremely simple, but delicious.

Before cooking clams (and other bivalve shellfish, like cockles) they must be left in a basin full of slightly salted, cold water for quite some time to allow the clams to eliminate all traces of sand; the water should be changed two or three times. Some suggest putting a plate upside down on the bottom of the basin so that all the sand released will collect under it. There is no need to add salt when cooking molluscs because of their lengthy soak in salted water; however, if you feel you cannot do without it then you can add a little at the same time as the pepper.

AMÊIJOAS NA CATAPLANA

Clams in a 'cataplana' ☞*Algarve*

Clams, 1 Kg; 2 1/4 lb
1 onion
Lean, smoked prosciutto ham
   (in one slice), 50 g; 1 3/4 oz
Chouriço (see Explanations),
   50 g; 1 3/4 oz
Mild, ground pimiento
Piri-piri (see Explanations)
Parsley
Pepper
Olive oil

Serves:	8
Preparation:	6'
Cooking:	20'
Difficulty:	●
Flavour:	● ● ●
Kcal (per serving):	202
Proteins (per serving):	11
Fats (per serving):	19
Nutritional value:	● ● ●

Before cooking, prepare the clams by soaking them in cold water (changing the water a couple of times) so that they eliminate all traces of sand and impurities (see note on previous page). Peel the onion, cut it into thin slices and slowly sauté it in the *cataplana* with 2-3 tablespoons of oil, the *piri-piri* without its seeds and crumbled into tiny pieces, a sprinkling of pepper and a dash of ground pimiento. When the onion becomes transparent, add the diced ham, the finely chopped *chouriço*, the clams and a sprig of parsley. Close the lid of the *cataplana* and cook slowly for 20 minutes. Open the *cataplana*, discard any shells that have not opened and serve immediately.

A cataplana is a cooking vessel typical of the Algarve region, though it is used in other regions in Portugal as well. Convex in shape, made of galvanised copper and with a lid that closes hermetically, it is ideal for slow-cooking dishes such as shellfish, rice, meat and fish. It can be found in shops that store special kitchen utensils. A pressure-cooker may be used in its place but, while the cooking time will be naturally shorter with this, it cannot be used in the oven, whereas a cataplana can; however, even any other type of heavy pot may be used, preferably made of earthenware and with a firmly fitting lid, which may be tied down with string if necessary.

CEBOLINHAS DE ESCABECHE

Pickled onions ☛ *Madeira*

Baby onions, 1 Kg; 2 ¹/₄ lb
Bay leaf
Cloves
Jamaica peppercorns
  (see page 61)
Piri-piri (see Explanations)
Coarse salt
Red wine vinegar

Serves:	8
Preparation:	10' + 72h
Cooking:	10'
Difficulty:	●
Flavour:	● ●
Kcal (per serving):	31
Proteins (per serving):	1
Fats (per serving):	0
Nutritional value:	●

Remove the outer skins and the roots of the onions then blanch them for about 10 minutes in plenty of salted, boiling water. Drain and allow to dry completely before putting them in an earthenware or glass pickling jar with a hermetic lid. Season with a pinch of salt and cover them completely with vinegar; add a bay leaf, about 10 Jamaica peppercorns, 2-3 cloves and the *piri-piri*, that is, a whole red pimiento. Cover the jar and keep for at least three days. These pickled onions are usually served as hors-d'œuvre but they are also delicious as an accompaniment to boiled meats or fish.

CENOURAS EM CONSERVA

Carrots in vinegar ☞ *Algarve*

3 carrots (4 if small)
4 cloves of garlic
Parsley
Mild, ground pimiento
Black olives in brine
(optional)
1 clove (optional)
Red wine vinegar
Salt

Serves:	6
Preparation:	15'+3h
Cooking:	12'
Difficulty:	●
Flavour:	● ●
Kcal (per serving):	17
Proteins (per serving):	1
Fats (per serving):	0
Nutritional value:	●

Rinse and peel the carrots then blanch them for 12 minutes in plenty of salted water. Drain them, leave them to cool, slice them into 7-8 mm (½ inch) thick rounds then put them in a bowl with a full glass of vinegar, the peeled and finely chopped garlic, a sprig of parsley (chopped), a teaspoon of ground pimiento and, if desired, a crushed clove. Store in the fridge for at least three hours, stirring the carrots every now and then.
Arrange the carrot rounds on a platter and serve with pitted black olives (if desired) as an appetiser.

CHOQUINHOS FRITOS COM TINTA

Baby cuttlefish fried with their ink sacs ☞ *Algarve*

Baby cuttlefish, 800 g; 1 ³/₄ lb
4 cloves of garlic
Bay leaf
Lettuce and cherry tomatoes
   (for accompaniment)
Salt and pepper
Olive oil

Serves: 6	
Preparation: 20'	
Cooking: 30'	
Difficulty: ● ●	
Flavour: ● ●	
Kcal (per serving): 311	
Proteins (per serving): 17	
Fats (per serving): 27	
Nutritional value: ● ● ●	

Rinse the cuttlefish well; prepare them by removing the cuttlebones, cartilage, etc., without separating the heads from the tentacles and, above all, making sure the ink sacs remain intact inside. Gently sauté the peeled cloves of garlic and a bay leaf in a pan (with a lid) containing half a glass of oil; add the dried cuttlefish, place the lid on the pan and cook over medium-low heat, stirring occasionally, for about 10 minutes, until the cuttlefish become red in colour.

At this point, add a pinch each of salt and pepper, put the lid back on the pan and cook for about 20 minutes, until the oil becomes transparent again like it was at the beginning.

Remove the cuttlefish with a draining spoon, leave to drain on kitchen paper then arrange them on a bed of lettuce on a platter, with cherry tomatoes as garnish.

MEXILHÕES À MODA DE AVEIRO

Fried mussels on skewers ☛ *Beira Litoral*

Mussels, 1 Kg; 2 ¹/4 lb
Bay leaf
2 cloves
Plain flour, 30 g; 1 oz; ¹/4 cup
White wine vinegar
Cherry tomatoes
   (for accompaniment)
Salt and pepper
Olive oil
Frying oil

Serves: 8	
Preparation: 15'+8h+48h	
Cooking: 10'	
Difficulty: ● ●	
Flavour: ● ●	
Kcal (per serving): 433	
Proteins (per serving): 8	
Fats (per serving): 37	
Nutritional value: ● ● ●	

Pour a full glass of vinegar into a bowl, add a tablespoon of olive oil, a bay leaf, a pinch each of salt and pepper, and the cloves. Cover and leave to stand for at least 6-8 hours, stirring occasionally. When the marinade is ready, prepare the mussels by scraping their shells and eliminating the beards that emerge, rinse them well but do not dry them, then put them into a large pan with a lid and allow them to open over intense heat without adding water or oil. Remove the mussels from their shells, drain and dry them carefully. Toss the mussels into flour to coat then thread 3-4 at a time on wooden skewers. Deep-fry the skewers in hot frying oil, remove them when golden crisp (about 5 minutes) then leave them to dry on kitchen paper. Arrange the fried skewers at the bottom of a fairly deep dish, pour the marinade over them then leave them there to marinate for at least 48 hours, basting them with the marinade liquid every now and then. Serve the skewered mussels together with cherry tomatoes as hors-d'œuvre.

Ovos Verdes

Egg and parsley croquettes ☞ *Estremadura*

9 eggs plus one egg-white
Parsley
Plain flour, 30 g; 1 oz; $^1/_4$ cup
Mixed salad greens
  (for serving)
Salt and pepper
Butter, 30 g; 1 oz; 2 tbsp
Frying oil

Serves:	8
Preparation:	15'
Cooking:	30'
Difficulty:	● ●
Flavour:	● ●
Kcal (per serving):	454
Proteins (per serving):	11
Fats (per serving):	37
Nutritional value:	● ● ●

Put 8 eggs in a pan full of cold water, bring to the boil and cook for 7 minutes; drain the hard-boiled eggs, allow to cool slightly then shell them. Slice the eggs into two lengthwise, scoop out the yolks and put them into a bowl; squash the yolks to a paste with the back of a fork and blend in a sprig of parsley (chopped), the butter (softened), salt and pepper.

Fill the cavities in the boiled eggs with mounds of this mixture then coat them with flour. Beat the remaining egg together with the raw egg-white and dip the floured eggs into it; deep-fry until golden crisp, drain then serve on a bed of mixed salad greens as hors-d'œuvre.

PEIXINHOS DA HORTA

Fried string beans ☞ *Estremadura*

Top and tail the beans and remove any filaments (cut into two if they are too long); blanch for 3-4 minutes in slightly salted water, drain and keep to one side. Put the flour and a pinch of salt in a bowl, add a glass of cold water (mixed with a drop of wine if desired), or at least a sufficient amount to obtain a smooth, soft batter using a hand mixer; blend in the egg and the finely chopped onion then leave to one side for about 30 minutes.

Dip the beans in the batter and leave them there for a few minutes before deep-frying them (a few at a time) in hot oil; drain and dry on kitchen paper. Sprinkle with salt and serve hot with wedges of lemon.

Although any type of green bean can be used, the original Portuguese recipe foresees the use of young, green Lima beans in their pods.

String (French) beans, 500 g;
1 lb 2 oz
Plain flour, 100 g; 4 oz; $3/4$ cup
1 egg
1 quarter of an onion
Dry white wine (optional)
1 lemon (for garnish)
Salt
Frying oil

Serves: 6	
Preparation: 15'+30'	
Cooking: 20'	
Difficulty: ● ●	
Flavour: ● ●	
Kcal (per serving): 339	
Proteins (per serving): 38	
Fats (per serving): 42	
Nutritional value: ● ● ●	

PATANISCAS DE BACALHAU

Dried codfish fritters ☞ *Estremadura*

Dried codfish, previously
soaked, 800 g; 1 1/4 lb
Plain flour, 150 g; 5-6 oz;
　1 1/3 cup
1 onion
1 egg
Full milk, 2 dl; 4 fl oz
2 lemons (one of which
　for garnish)
Parsley
Salt and pepper
Frying oil, olive oil

Serves: 8	
Preparation: 15'+2h15'	
Cooking: 15'	
Difficulty: ●●●	
Flavour: ●●	
Kcal (per serving): 470	
Proteins (per serving): 20	
Fats (per serving): 37	
Nutritional value: ●●●	

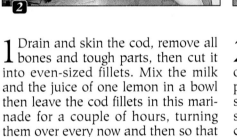

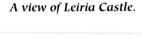

A view of Leiria Castle.

1 Drain and skin the cod, remove all bones and tough parts, then cut it into even-sized fillets. Mix the milk and the juice of one lemon in a bowl then leave the cod fillets in this marinade for a couple of hours, turning them over every now and then so that they absorb the flavour all through.

2 Using a hand-mixer, whisk the flour, egg, one tablespoon of olive oil, and a pinch each of salt and pepper together in a large bowl, adding sufficient water to obtain a thick, smooth batter; blend in the finely chopped onion and parsley.

3 Drain the cod fillets of the marinade, flake them and add to the batter; mix then leave to stand for 15 minutes. Deep-fry the *pataniscas* by dropping tablespoons of the batter and cod mixture into hot frying oil.

4 As soon as they become golden crisp, remove the fritters from the oil with a draining spoon, dry on kitchen paper and sprinkle with a little salt. Serve hot with wedges of lemon as an hors-d'oeuvre.

SANTOLA NO CARRO

Stuffed crab ☞ *Douro*

2 crabs, approx. 800 g
  (1 ³/₄ lb) each
Wholemeal breadcrumbs,
  300 g; 12 oz; 2 ¹/₂ cups
1 onion
Parsley (plus
  some for garnish)
Hot, ground pimiento
Dry Port
Cherry tomatoes (for garnish)
Salt and pepper
Olive oil

Serves:	6
Preparation:	25'
Cooking:	15'
Difficulty:	● ●
Flavour:	● ●
Kcal (per serving):	369
Proteins (per serving):	14
Fats (per serving):	10
Nutritional value:	● ●

1 Rinse the crabs and blanch them for 5-6 minutes in a pan full of slightly salted, boiling water. Remove them from the pan and keep the cooking liquid; when cold, prise the two shells of each crab apart with a pointed but blunt utensil, being careful not to crack the shells since they must be kept. Remove the flesh from the belly shell of each crab and discard the sacs that contain sandy material near the heads. Prepare the onion, chop it and sauté it in a pan with 2-3 tablespoons of oil until golden; remove the pan from the heat and blend in the crab flesh, the breadcrumbs, a chopped sprig of parsley, and a pinch each of salt, pepper and ground pimiento. Put the pan back on the stove at high heat, add half a glass of Port and allow the flavours to blend a couple of minutes while stirring. Transfer the mixture into a bowl.

2 Fill the belly shells with spoonfuls of the mixture and smooth the surface of each; place the dorsal shells back in place and put the reassembled crabs in the oven, preheated to 140°C (250-300°F), until the stuffing heats through without browning. Serve the warm crabs *no carro* (meaning: in their shells) with sprigs of parsley and cherry tomatoes.

RICE DISHES, BROTHS AND SOUPS

Simple, hearty and full of imagination:
three adjectives that describe the essence
of Lusitanian cooking and which are particularly
evident in this chapter. Besides a recipe
for the famous Caldo verde, you'll find many others
straight from the heart of Portuguese tradition,
dishes that demonstrate just how much
can be achieved with genuine, familiar
and humble ingredients. Rice and bread are
the most popular ingredients: both are employed
in versatile combinations with fish, shellfish
and seafood, meat and salami, or even pulses,
herbs and vegetables. A compendium of recipes
suitable for any occasion, and since many
can be considered all-in-one meals they even
fulfil present-day dietary requirements.

2

ARROZ DE BACALHAU

Rice with dried codfish ☞ *Douro*

Risotto rice, 300 g; 12 oz; 2 1/2 cups	
Dried codfish, unsoaked, 500 g; 1 lb 2 oz	
1 onion	
3 ripe cooking tomatoes	
Olive oil	

Serves:	4
Preparation:	10'
Cooking:	45'
Difficulty:	● ●
Flavour:	● ● ●
Kcal (per serving):	469
Proteins (per serving):	27
Fats (per serving):	10
Nutritional value:	● ●

1 Contrary to the normal use of dried codfish, in this recipe it must not be soaked beforehand but simply rinsed well in cold, running water then skinned and cut into bite-size pieces. Peel the onion, slice it thinly then sauté it gently in a casserole (preferably earthenware) with 3-4 tablespoons of oil. Add the codfish and allow the flavours to blend for about ten minutes; rinse the tomatoes, remove their seeds, then add them to the casserole over lowest heat to simmer for a further ten minutes, pressing them with the back of a wooden spoon to reduce them to a pulp.

2 Pour approximately 2 litres (1 2/3 pints) of water into the casserole and bring to the boil; add the rice (there is no need to add salt) and cook over low heat until it is cooked but not too soft (*al dente*) and most of the liquid has been absorbed. Remember to stir the ingredients every now and then to avoid them sticking to the pan. ✱

ARROZ DE BERBIGÃO

Rice with seafood ☞ *Algarve*

1 Soak the molluscs in cold water (changing it at least twice) to eliminate all traces of sand and impurities. Once clean, rinse the *berbigões* well and put them, still wet, into a *cataplana* (see page 11) or similar cooking vessel; close the lid and allow them to open over very low heat. Remove them from the cataplana, drain and keep in a warm place; filter and keep the liquid. Cut the peeled garlic into thin slices and sauté it slowly in the *cataplana* with 5-6 tablespoons of oil. Add the filtered cockle liquid, a sprig of fresh coriander (tied) and sufficient slightly salted water to cook the rice (to a total of approx. 1.5 litres; 2 ½ pints). Bring to the boil and cook for about 5 minutes.

2 Remove the coriander, add the rice, season to taste with salt and pepper then cover the *cataplana*; simmer as slowly as possible for just under 15 minutes until the rice has absorbed almost all the liquid (the cata-

plana may be put in the oven at 180°C (350°F), but cooking time will naturally be double). Remove the pan from the heat, take the lid off, cover the rice with the *berbigões* and sprinkle with freshly ground pepper and chopped parsley. Serve immediately.

The berbigão *(plural:* berbigões*) is a bivalve mollusc (*cerastoderma edule, *similar to the* cardium edule*). The shell is dull ivory in colour, rounded and with convex radial ribs, whereas the flesh is yellowish.*
In Spain it is called berberecho, *in France* bucaude *(or* coque*) and in Great Britain a* cockle *(or* little clam*). If these are difficult to find they may be substituted with other small edible molluscs.*

Risotto or timbale rice, 300 g; 12 oz; 2 ½ cups
Berbigões (see below), 1 Kg; 2 ¼ lb
4-5 cloves of garlic
Fresh coriander
Parsley
Salt and pepper
Olive oil

Serves:	4
Preparation:	10'
Cooking:	30'
Difficulty:	● ●
Flavour:	● ●
Kcal (per serving):	469
Proteins (per serving):	20
Fats (per serving):	14
Nutritional value:	● ●

Arroz de Cabidela

Rice with chicken ☞ *Beira Alta*

Risotto or timbale rice, 300 g;
  12 oz; 2 ¹/₂ cups
1 chicken, ready for use,
  approx. 1.2 Kg; 2 ³/₄ lb
1 onion
1 clove of garlic
Bay leaf and parsley
Carqueja (see opposite page)
Tomato paste concentrate
  (optional)
Red wine vinegar
Salt and pepper
Olive oil

Serves:	4
Preparation:	15'
Cooking:	50'
Difficulty:	● ●
Flavour:	● ●
Kcal (per serving):	623
Proteins (per serving):	32
Fats (per serving):	27
Nutritional value:	● ● ●

1 Cut the chicken into small pieces (about 20) and place them in a casserole (preferably earthenware with a lid) with 3-4 tablespoons of oil, the peeled onion cut into pieces, the peeled and crushed clove of garlic, a bay leaf, a sprig each of parsley and *carqueja* leaves, and a pinch each of salt and pepper. Cover the casserole with its lid and cook slowly over very low heat for about 30 minutes, adding a little water whenever necessary to keep the meat moist.

2 Pour 1.5 litres (2 ¹/₂ pints) of water into the casserole, put the lid back on and bring to the boil. Uncover, add the rice, cover once more and cook slowly until almost all the liquid has been absorbed (about 20 minutes), stirring every now and then.

3 A few minutes before the end of cooking time, add half a glass of vinegar, mixed with a tablespoon of tomato paste, if desired. Mix to blend the flavours and as soon as the rice begins to boil once more, remove the casserole from the heat and serve immediately. This is one of the many Portuguese first courses that can also be served as an all-in-one meal.

Panorama of Manteigas, a town on the outskirts of Guarda.

Carqueja (genistella trilobata) is a short shrub of the Broom family common in Portugal (and in certain areas of Spain as well, where it is known as carqueisa): its aromatic leaves are used in many dishes but its woody stalks are also used as fragrant kindling wood for barbecues. It can be either substituted with thyme, or omitted altogether.

The traditional recipe actually calls for chicken blood mixed with the vinegar, instead of tomato paste; however, even a teaspoon of mild, ground pimiento can take its place.

AÇORDA DE CAMARÃO

Bread and scampi soup ☛ *Estremadura*

Scampi (or king prawns),
  1 Kg; 2 1/4 lb
5-6 slices of stale farmhouse
  bread
3 cloves of garlic
2 egg yolks
Ground hot pimiento
Parsley
Dry white wine
Salt and pepper
Olive oil

Serves: 4	
Preparation: 20'	
Cooking: 1h	
Difficulty: ● ●	
Flavour: ● ● ●	
Kcal (per serving): 526	
Proteins (per serving): 44	
Fats (per serving): 31	
Nutritional value: ● ● ●	

1 Rinse the scampi well and blanch them briefly in approximately 2 litres (3¼ pints) of slightly salted boiling water with a sprig of parsley and a drop of wine. Drain them (keeping the liquid) and shell all but four of them (to be used as garnish), removing the intestinal vein. Keep the scampi tails in a warm place. Put the heads and the shells with the claws attached back into the broth and simmer for about 30 minutes. Filter the broth obtained through a fine sieve into a soup tureen; add the cubed bread.

2 Sauté the peeled and finely sliced cloves of garlic in a large casserole (preferably earthenware) with 4-5 tablespoon of oil; as soon as it becomes golden in colour, add the broth with the bread, stir carefully and allow the flavours to blend. When the bread has disintegrated to a soft, smooth mush consistency, season with salt, pepper and a pinch of ground pimiento. Add the scampi tails, mix with care then remove from the heat. Leave to cool for a few minutes, then gently blend in the egg yolks. Serve the *açorda* garnished with the 4 remaining scampi and tiny sprigs of parsley.

CALDO DE CEBOLA

Onion and potato soup ☞ *Trás-os-Montes*

4 potatoes (medium sized)
3 onions
Salpicão, (see Explanations)
  100 g (4 oz) in one piece
Salt
Olive oil

Serves: 4	
Preparation: 10'	
Cooking: 35'	
Difficulty: ●	
Flavour: ● ● ●	
Kcal (per serving): 357	
Proteins (per serving): 13	
Fats (per serving): 17	
Nutritional value: ● ●	

This is a delicious but simple and nutritious soup. Peel the potatoes and boil them in plenty of slightly salted water (approx. 2 litres; 3¼ pints)) with 2-3 tablespoons of oil and the piece of *salpicão*. Keeping the pot on the heat, remove and drain the potatoes and keep them in a warm place; add the peeled and quartered onions to the stock in the pot and cook slowly, seasoning with salt to taste. Put a boiled potato (or more if small) and a few slices of cooked *salpicão* into individual soup dishes then add the onions and broth. Serve immediately. And what can be served as a second course? Nothing, really, since the soup is actually a first and second course, plus vegetables.

CALDO VERDE

Potato and cabbage soup 〜 *Minho*

Couve gallega (or savoy
   cabbage), 500 g; 1 lb 2 oz
4 potatoes (medium sized)
1 onion
2-3 cloves of garlic
Chouriço, (see Explanations)
   200 g; 8 oz
Fresh parsley or coriander
   (for garnish)
Salt
Olive oil

Serves:	4
Preparation:	20'
Cooking:	30'
Difficulty:	● ●
Flavour:	● ●
Kcal (per serving):	436
Proteins (per serving):	20
Fats (per serving):	23
Nutritional value:	● ●

Prepare the cabbage by removing the core and the tough outer leaves; rinse it well, drain and separate the leaves. Peel the onion, cloves of garlic and potatoes. Cut the potatoes and onion into pieces and put them into a casserole (preferably earthenware with a lid) with the garlic and 2-3 tablespoons of oil. Cover with water (about 1.5 litres; 2^1/$_2$ pints), bring to the boil, cover and simmer for 15 minutes. In the meantime, roll up the cabbage leaves and slice them, one after the other, as thinly as possible. When the ingredients in the casserole are cooked, use an immersion blender to cream the potatoes, garlic and onion (or remove them from the casserole and pass them through a vegetable mill back into the casserole). Add the cabbage, the sliced *chouriço* and a pinch of salt; bring to the boil once more, cover and simmer for just less than 15 minutes. Serve the soup hot, garnished with sprigs of parsley or fresh coriander; if wished, a drop of raw oil may be added to each plate.

CANJA DE CONQUILHAS

Rice in arselle (wedge clam) broth ☞ *Algarve*

Soup rice, 180 g; 7 oz; 1³/₄ cups
Arselle/wedge clams, 1 Kg;
  2 ¹/₄ lb
2 egg yolks
1 onion
1 lemon
Parsley
Salt
Olive oil

Serves: 4	
Preparation: 15′	
Cooking: 25′	
Difficulty: ● ●	
Flavour: ●	
Kcal (per serving): 415	
Proteins (per serving): 21	
Fats (per serving): 18	
Nutritional value: ● ● ●	

1 Prepare the wedge clams for use (see page 10), put them in a pan, add water to cover, put the lid on and allow the shells to open over high heat. Remove the pan from the heat and discard any clams that have failed to open; filter the cooking liquid and keep to one side. Peel and finely chop the onion together with a sprig of parsley, and sauté in a casserole (preferably earthenware) with 4-5 tablespoons of oil.

2 Pour the clam broth (adding hot water if it is insufficient) into a pot, add salt to taste and bring to the boil; add the rice and boil until cooked but not soft (*al dente*) and most of the liquid has been absorbed. Remove the pot from the heat and allow to cool for a few minutes; whisk the egg yolks with the juice of the lemon and the chopped parsley and blend into the soup. Serve immediately. What happens to the wedge clams? They'll be a delicious hors-d'œuvre! This *canja* can be made with shrimp broth as well, or even with that of dried codfish, the way they make it in other regions in the country.

MIGAS À ALENTEJANA

Mixed pork mush ☞ *Alentejo*

Pork spare-ribs, 400 g;
   12 oz-1 lb
Boned saddle of pork, 300 g;
   10-12 oz
Lard or unsmoked bacon,
   100 g; 4 oz
Unsalted farmhouse bread,
   600 g; 1 1/4 lb
3-4 cloves of garlic
Ground hot pimiento, salt

Serves: 4	
Preparation: 15'+8 h	
Cooking: 20'	
Difficulty: ●	
Flavour: ● ● ●	
Kcal (per serving): 812	
Proteins (per serving): 36	
Fats (per serving): 34	
Nutritional value: ● ● ●	

1 Peel the cloves of garlic and pound them to a paste in a mortar (or in a blender) and add 2 teaspoons of ground pimiento; rub this paste all over the spare-ribs and pork, put them in a bowl, cover and keep to one side for 8 hours.

2 Chop the spare-rib meat and pork into small pieces and cube the bacon; put these ingredients into a casserole (preferably earthenware) with just enough water to cover them. Sauté until evenly browned then remove all meats from the casserole; filter the remaining fat and gravy through a fine sieve and keep to one side. Cut the bread into pieces and put them in a large bowl; add a little lukewarm water and crumble the bread, without making a pulp. Put the crumbled bread into a frying pan, add a little of the filtered fat, adjust for salt and, stirring, gently sauté until the bread becomes nicely browned. Transfer the fried bread to a serving dish, moisten with the remaining fat and arrange the cooked meats over it. This, too, is an all-in-one dish.

MIGAS DE PÃO DE MILHO

Corn-bread and garlic mush ☛ *Ribatejo*

1 Cut the cornbread into slices and put them in a large casserole (preferably earthenware) and enough slightly salted boiling water to just cover. Bring to the boil and cook for 5-6 minutes; remove the casserole from the stove and drain off the water. Using a wooden mallet, gently pound the soaked cornbread left in the casserole, crumbling it, but not to a pulp.

2 Make a well (about 10 cm; 3³/4 inches in diameter) in the middle of the crumbled bread, put the peeled and roughly chopped garlic into this, then fill the well with oil; pour a little oil over the surrounding bread as well. Put the casserole back over low heat, bring to the boil and cook for 5 minutes, stirring all the time. Smooth the surface of the *migas* and serve accompanied by olives in brine. This is delicious served with grilled sardines (see page 63).

This dish is delicious and extremely simple to make, and conforms to modern dietary recommendations. However, there is a little secret in the original recipe: the wooden mallet used in the Ribatejo is made of orangewood, and is called a pé de chibo (goat hoof) because that is the actual shape of the utensil. Instead of cornbread, broa (see page 34) may be used if preferred.

Stale cornbread, 500 g;
  1 lb 2 oz
3 cloves of garlic
Olives in brine
  (for accompaniment)
Salt
Olive oil

Serves:	4
Preparation:	5′
Cooking:	10′
Difficulty:	●
Flavour:	● ● ●
Kcal (per serving):	478
Proteins (per serving):	10
Fats (per serving):	16
Nutritional value:	● ●

PASTÉIS DE MOLHO

Parcels in clear broth ☛ *Beira Baixa*

For the dough:
1 whole egg + 1 yolk
Plain flour, 300 g; 12 oz;
   2 1/2 cups (plus extra for
   the pastry board)
Cooking fat (or butter),
   approx. 100 g; 4 oz
Salt

For the stuffing:
Lean minced beef, 300 g;
   12 oz
1 onion
Parsley
Saffron (in strands)
Red wine vinegar
Salt and pepper
Olive oil

Serves:	6
Preparation:	40'+30'
Cooking:	35'
Difficulty:	● ●
Flavour:	● ●
Kcal (per serving):	809
Proteins (per serving):	29
Fats (per serving):	41
Nutritional value:	● ● ●

1 Put the flour into a bowl and blend in (using a hand mixer) the egg, the yolk, a pinch of salt and sufficient water to obtain a stiff, smooth dough; keep to one side until the stuffing (next step) has been prepared.

2 Peel and finely chop the onion. Sauté it until soft in a pan with 3-4 tablespoons of oil, add the minced meat, a pinch each of salt and pepper, and gently brown for about 12 minutes. Leave to cool.

3 Roll out the dough to a disk on a floured pastry board and brush it all over with melted fat; roll up the disk to a cylinder and knead by hand to incorporate the fat. This step must be repeated three times. Thereafter, roll out the dough once more, but without greasing it this time. Roll up to a cylinder again and leave to stand for 30 minutes.

4 Cut the cylinder of dough into 6 disks about 1.5 cm (3/4 inch) thick; grease them with oil and roll them out to 16-18 cm (6 1/2-7 1/2 inches) diameter disks on the pastry board. In the centre of each disk put a ball of stuffing the size of an apricot; fold the disk over in two and seal the edges. Place the *pastéis* on a greased oven tray, bake in the oven preheated to 200°C (375-400°F) for 15 minutes, then cool on a rack. In the meantime, boil approximately 1.5 litres (2 1/2 pints) of water for 10 minutes with 3 tablespoons of vinegar, a pinch of salt, a sprig of parsley and a pinch of saffron strands. Place a parcel in each soup dish, cover with the filtered broth and serve immediately garnished with sprigs of parsley.

The gardens of what was formerly the Bishop's Palace, Castelo Branco.

RANCHO À MODA DO MINHO

Chickpea and pork soup ☛ *Minho*

Small pasta for soups, 120 g; 5 oz;
    1 cup
Shin of beef, 250 g; 9 oz
Unsmoked bacon (in one piece),
    250 g; 9 oz
Chouriço (see Explanations),
    250 g; 9 oz
Chickpeas, 350 g; 3/4 lb
3-4 potatoes, 2 onions
Ground pimiento
Salt and pepper
Cooking fat, 20 g; 3/4 oz;1 1/2 tbsp
Olive oil

Serves: 6	
Preparation: 10'+6h	
Cooking: 2h 15'	
Difficulty: ● ●	
Flavour: ● ●	
Kcal (per serving): 966	
Proteins (per serving): 43	
Fats (per serving): 56	
Nutritional value: ● ● ●	

The imposing flight of steps that lead to the Bom Jesus do Monte church in Braga.

1 Soak the chickpeas in water for about 6 hours before start-ing to prepare the meal. Drain them and put them into a casserole (preferably earthenware with a lid) together with the shin of beef, the bacon, and *chouriço* in fairly long pieces; cov-er with plenty of cold water, season with salt and pepper, cover and bring to the boil; simmer for a couple of hours.

2 In the meantime, peel and finely chop the onions; slowly melt the cooking fat in 5-6 tablespoons of oil in another pan and gently sauté the onions. Keep in a warm place.

3 Test the meats and salami to see if they are tender; if so, re-move them from the casserole and drain. Bone the shin of beef and cut it and the bacon into small pieces, and slice the *chouriço* into rounds. Put all the meats back into the casserole with the chickpeas and add the onions with their fat, the pasta, and the peeled and cubed potatoes; add a pinch of ground pimiento and taste for salt and pepper. When the potatoes and pasta are cooked but not too soft (*al dente*) remove the *rancho* from the stove and serve piping hot.

SOPA DA BEIRA

Maize-flour and cabbage soup ☞ *Beira Alta*

Maize-flour ('polenta'), 200 g; 8 oz; 1 3/4 cups	
Half a green cabbage	
1 bunch of turnip tops	
1 large piece of prosciutto ham bone (with some ham and fat attached)	
Salt and pepper, olive oil	

Serves:	4
Preparation:	15'
Cooking:	2h
Difficulty:	● ●
Flavour:	● ●
Kcal (per serving):	288
Proteins (per serving):	6
Fats (per serving):	10
Nutritional value:	● ●

1 Put the ham bone (sawn into two if very long) into a large casserole (preferably earthenware with a lid) with approximately 2 litres (3 1/4 pints) of unsalted water; bring to the boil, cover, lower the heat to minimum and simmer for one hour. In the meantime, rinse both the cabbage and turnip tops well; drain and allow to dry. Separate the cabbage leaves, selecting the best ones, and roughly chop them (this is best done by hand) together with the selected turnip tops.

2 When the ham bone is ready, remove it and scrape all the meat and fat back into the broth; add the chopped greens, salt and pepper to taste and 2-3 tablespoons of oil. Continue to cook over low heat, with the lid on, for about 30 minutes, then add the maize-flour previously blended with a little cold water; increase the heat a little and cook without a lid, stirring all the time, until the soup is thick and creamy. Serve immediately.

SOPA DE CAÇÃO

Skate soup ☛ *Alentejo*

Skate fillets, 500 g; 1 lb 2 oz
6-8 slices of stale farmhouse
 bread
3 cloves of garlic
Bay leaves and fresh
 coriander
Ground, mild pimiento
Plain flour, 15 g; 1 oz; 1 tbsp
White wine vinegar
Salt
Olive oil

Serves: 4-6	
Preparation: 10'+2h	
Cooking: 20'	
Difficulty: ●	
Flavour: ● ●	
Kcal (per serving): 406	
Proteins (per serving): 21	
Fats (per serving): 12	
Nutritional value: ● ●	

1 Skin the skate fillets and remove any bones and tough parts. Put them in a bowl with 2 glasses of vinegar, the same amount of water, a pinch of salt and the bay leaves; leave the fish to marinate for a couple of hours, turning them over every now and then. Peel the cloves of garlic and sauté them until soft with a chopped sprig of coriander in a casserole (preferably earthenware) with 3-4 tablespoons of oil; add about 1.5 litres (2½ pints) of cold water, bring to the boil then add the skate fillets.

2 Blend the flour with a glass of vinegar and a teaspoon of ground pimiento and add to the casserole; lower the heat and simmer slowly until the fillets and the flour sauce are cooked. Cut the slices of bread in half and place them in a soup tureen; first pour the skate broth over the bread then arrange the fillets on top; serve immediately. This can be served as an all-in-one meal.

SOPA DE LANGUEIRÃO

Razor-clam soup ☞ *Algarve*

Razor-clams, 2 dozen
Soup rice, 150 g; 6 oz;
   1 ¹/₃ cups
1 onion
2-3 ripe cooking tomatoes
Parsley
Salt and pepper
Olive oil

Serves:	4
Preparation:	20′
Cooking:	45′
Difficulty:	●●
Flavour:	●●
Kcal (per serving):	340
Proteins (per serving):	15
Fats (per serving):	12
Nutritional value:	●●

1 Rinse the razor-shells well under running water and put them, dripping wet, into a pan with a little water; cover the pan and allow them to open over medium heat. Remove the pan from the heat, remove the razor-shells, drain, then extract the flesh from the shells; put the shell-fish morsels back into the pan containing the broth and cook for a further 4-5 minutes. Thereafter, scoop them out, put them in a colander, rinse thoroughly under cold, running water to eliminate all traces of sand and put them aside; filter the cooking liquid through a fine sieve and keep this as well.

2 Peel and finely chop the onion, sauté it slowly in a casserole (preferably earthenware with a lid) with 2-3 tablespoons of oil and a sprig of parsley.

3 Rinse the tomatoes, remove the seeds and roughly chop; add these to the casserole and simmer gently, stirring every now and then, for about 10 minutes or until the tomatoes are soft.

4 Add sufficient hot water to the filtered cooking liquid to make up 1.5 litres (2¹/₂ pints) and pour over the tomatoes; add the razor-shell morsels and salt and pepper to taste. Bring to the boil, add the rice and cook, allowing the rice to absorb a good amount of the liquid. Serve immediately.

This soup can be prepared without adding tomatoes: when the rice is cooked, remove the pot from the stove and add two egg yolks beaten with lemon juice to the sopa, as in the recipe for Açorda de camarão given on page 28.

SOPA DE FEIJÃO-MANTEIGA

Bean and vegetable soup ☞ *Algarve*

Lima (or haricot) beans, fresh
  or frozen, 200 g; 8 oz; 1 cup
4 potatoes
2 sweet potatoes
Yellow pumpkin (in one slice),
  150 g; 5-6 oz
1 onion
Parsley
Salt
Olive oil

Serves: 4-6	
Preparation: 10'	
Cooking: 1h	
Difficulty: ● ●	
Flavour: ● ●	
Kcal (per serving): 399	
Proteins (per serving): 11	
Fats (per serving): 13	
Nutritional value: ● ●	

If dry beans are being used they must be soaked for about 4-5 hours before starting to make the soup, then drain them and put them in a pot with plenty of cold water; bring to the boil, cover, lower the heat to minimum, simmer for 30 minutes then drain them, keeping the cooking liquid. Peel the pumpkin and both types of potatoes. Peel and chop the onion together with a sprig of parsley and sauté in a casserole (preferably earthenware) with 4-5 tablespoons of oil; add the drained beans, a pinch of salt, and cook over low heat for about 10 minutes. Cut the two types of potatoes into wedges, cube the pumpkin and add both to the casserole; cook until tender. If necessary, add a few tablespoons of the liquid in which the beans were boiled – not too much, because the *sopa* should be rather thick.

Dry red beans (kidney
  or similar), 200 g; 8 oz; 1 cup
Smoked bacon (one slice),
  150 g; 6 oz
Chouriço (see Explanations)
  in one piece, 100 g; 4 oz
4 potatoes
1 rib of celery
1 carrot
A quarter of a savoy cabbage
1 onion
1 clove of garlic
Fresh coriander
Bay leaf
Salt and pepper

Serves: 4-6	
Preparation: 20'+3h	
Cooking: 1h 20'	
Difficulty: ● ●	
Flavour: ● ●	
Kcal (per serving): 540	
Proteins (per serving): 22	
Fats (per serving): 26	
Nutritional value: ● ● ●	

SOPA DE PEDRA

Vegetable soup with cured meats ☞ *Ribatejo*

Soak the beans for 3 hours beforehand, then drain them and put them in a earthenware casserole together with the bacon, the *chouriço*, the peeled onion cut into wedges, the peeled and crushed clove of garlic, a bay leaf and salt and pepper. Cover with plenty of slightly salted water and bring to the boil; put the lid on the casserole and simmer for about one hour, or until the cured meats are tender. In the meantime, rinse and prepare the remaining vegetables. When the meats are cooked, remove them from the casserole and drain; while the broth is still simmering, add the cubed potatoes and carrot, the celery cut it into small pieces, the finely sliced cabbage and a sprig of fresh coriander. Simmer until all ingredients are tender. Remove the casserole from the stove, add the meats cut into pieces and serve sprinkled with chopped coriander.

The *sopa de pedra* is traditionally served with a well-washed smooth stone from the river at the bottom of the soup tureen.

A tale lies behind this dish with such a strange name. It narrates that a hungry wayfarer, on reaching a village and knocking on the door of one of the houses, asked: "Excuse me, I'd like to make some stone soup and since I've already got a stone from the river, and the water, I need a potato. Could you kindly give me one?" Then he knocked on a second door, saying: "Excuse me, I'd like to make some stone soup and since I've already got a stone from the river, the water and a potato, I need an onion. Could you kindly give me one?" And on he went, knocking at all the doors and getting a carrot, a clove of garlic, some cabbage, salt and a piece of ham rind to flavour the soup. Ending up with even a piece of bread. This way, the hungry wayfarer made himself a good, warm meal!

Sopa Rica de Peixe

Mixed fish soup ☛ *Estremadura*

Mixed, good quality fish
(frog fish, conger-eel, turbot,
skate), 1 Kg; 2 1/4 lb
1 medium-sized eel
Medium-sized cuttlefish or
squid, 400 g; 12 oz-1 lb
5 razor-shells
5 king prawns
5 scampi
Mussels, 500 g; 1 lb 2 oz
Clams, 500 g; 1 lb 2 oz
2 onions
2 cloves of garlic
1 sweet pepper
Saffron
Bouquet garni, tied (bay leaf,
parsley, piece of leek
cut julienne)
6-8 slices of toasted farmhouse
bread (for serving)
Dry white wine
Salt, pepper and
peppercorns
Olive oil

Serves: 6-8	
Preparation: 25'	
Cooking: 2h	
Difficulty: ● ● ●	
Flavour: ● ● ●	
Kcal (per serving): 538	
Proteins (per serving): 44	
Fats (per serving): 21	
Nutritional value: ● ●	

1 All fish, shellfish and seafood must be previously cleaned and prepared for use; separate the scampi and prawn heads from their tails, eliminating the intestines; blanch the cuttlefish in boiling water for 20 minutes, drain and slice into rings. Cut the fish into pieces, keeping the bones, fins and heads, since these (together with the heads of the seafood) will be used for the broth; if all these trimmings are not enough, bouillon cubes may be used.

2 Peel one of the onions and cut it into thin strips; sauté slowly in a casserole with 5 tablespoons of oil, add all the fish trimmings and simmer for about 10 minutes. Pour about 1.5 litres (2 1/2 pints) of water into the casserole, add salt to taste and 3-4 peppercorns; cover and simmer for approximately one hour.

3 In another casserole (preferably earthenware) sauté the peeled and crushed cloves of garlic with 5 tablespoons of oil; remove the garlic as soon as it colours then, in its place, sauté the other onion (prepared in the same way as the other) with the bouquet garni.

4 In the meantime, rinse the sweet pepper and remove its seeds and fibrous parts; cut it into thin slices and add these to the onion and bouquet garni in the second casserole. Cook slowly for 7-8 minutes. When the fish broth in the first casserole has cooked sufficiently, filter it and pour it into the casserole containing the sweet pepper; add a pinch of saffron and a glass of wine.

5 Add the cuttlefish and fish (frog fish, conger-eel, turbot, etc.), bring slowly to the boil then add the shellfish, seafood, and the eel cut into pieces. Cook over low heat until all ingredients are ready, adding salt and pepper to taste. Put the toasted bread at the bottom of a soup tureen and arrange all types of fish and seafood over them; remove the bouquet garni from the broth before pouring it into the tureen, then serve.

SOPA DE TRIGO

Wheat-grain soup ☛ *Madeira*

Wheat-grain, 150 g; 5-6 oz;
   1 1/4 cups
Uncured belly of pork, 300 g;
   12 oz
4 medium-sized potatoes
1 sweet potato
Dry haricot beans, 200 g; 8 oz;
   1 cup
Pumpkin (one slice), 200 g; 8 oz
Salt

Serves:	4-6
Preparation:	10'+5h
Cooking:	1h 10'
Difficulty:	● ●
Flavour:	● ●
Kcal (per serving):	893
Proteins (per serving):	19
Fats (per serving):	52
Nutritional value:	● ● ●

1 Both the wheat-grain and beans must be soaked in cold water 4-5 hours prior to starting the recipe. Drain them and put them into a large casserole (preferably earthenware with a lid) with the pork belly; add sufficient cold water to cover and season with salt to taste. Bring to the boil, put the lid on the casserole, lower the heat to minimum and simmer for at least 45 minutes.

2 Add the peeled and cubes potatoes, the peeled sweet potato left whole and the peeled and cubed pumpkin. Cook until tender (about 20 minutes). Remove the casserole from the stove, extract the bacon and cut it into small pieces and arrange these on a warm platter together with the sweet potato: these will be served as a second course. Serve the soup while hot, reducing it slightly on a fast boil if it is too liquid.

FRESH AND SALTED FISH; SHELLFISH, AND SEAFOOD

*Lusitanian cooking is proverbially rich
when it comes to fish; it's a real pity to have
to choose among so many excellent dishes
to select the best ones for you. One of these is
the famous Caldeirada, which is made
in practically every village along
the Portuguese shores, and every village
claims that its version is the best.
This chapter ends with a rich assortment
of recipes using dried codfish, the essence
of Portuguese cooking, like the celebrated
Bacalhau à Gomes de Sá, the pride
of Oporto. Many of the recipes described
in both the section on fresh fish and in that
on preserved fish are all-in-one dishes.*

3

ATUM COM TOMATE

Tuna with tomatoes ☞ *Algarve*

Tuna steak, approx. 7-800 g;
  1 1/2 - 1 3/4 lb
4 ripe cooking tomatoes
1 onion
2 cloves of garlic
1 clove
Bay leaf
Salt and pepper
Fresh salad of tomatoes
  and sweet peppers
  (for accompaniment)
Cooking fat, 10 g; 1/2 oz; 3/4 tbsp
Olive oil

Serves: 4	
Preparation: 10'	
Cooking: 30'	
Difficulty: ● ●	
Flavour: ● ●	
Kcal (per serving): 384	
Proteins (per serving): 44	
Fats (per serving): 17	
Nutritional value: ● ●	

Peel both the onion and garlic and cut into thin slices. Rinse the tomatoes, remove the seeds and slice. Oil the bottom of an earthenware casserole (with lid) and cover it with half of the sliced onion, garlic and tomatoes. Spear the tuna steak with the clove split in two and brush each side of the fish with the melted cooking fat; place it over the tomatoes and onion in the casserole, season with salt and pepper and add the bay leaf.

Cover with the remaining garlic, onion and tomato slices; cover the casserole and simmer over very low heat for about 30 minutes, removing the lid about 5-6 minutes before the end to reduce the sauce. Serve the tuna with its sauce and accompanied by a salad of fresh tomatoes and sweet peppers.

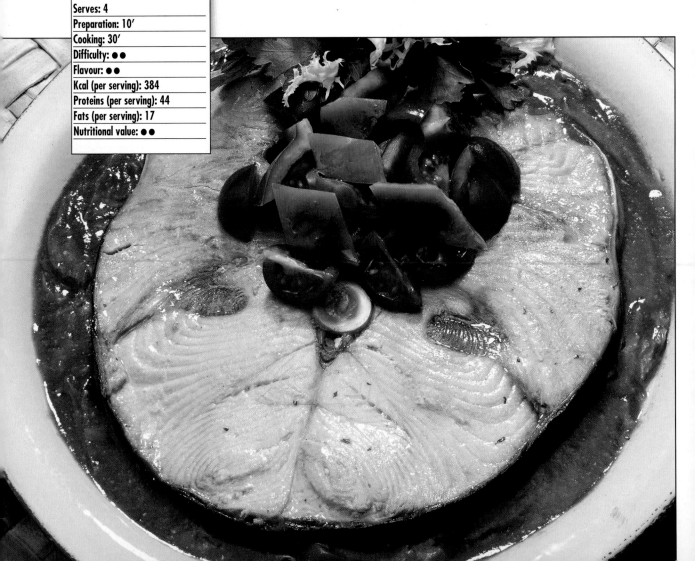

CALDEIRADA

Seafood stew ☞ *Algarve*

Before starting, eliminate all traces of sand and impurities in the clams by soaking them in water for some time, changing the water at least twice. Moreover, prepare the squids by removing the eyes, tooth, entrails and cartilage; rinse them then cut the bodies and tentacles into bite-size pieces (a hint: if the squids are medium-large, blanch them for about 10 minutes before cutting them – this will make them more tender). Following this, scale (if necessary) the fish and after rinsing them, cut them into pieces as well. Rinse the tomatoes, remove the seeds and cut into pieces. Peel the garlic and onions, finely slice and sauté slowly in a casserole (preferably earthenware with a lid) with 4-5 tablespoons of oil; add the tomatoes, a chopped sprig of parsley, the piri-piri without its seeds and crumbled; simmer for about ten minutes then add the fish and squids. Pour a full glass of wine over the simmering ingredients and add sufficient lukewarm water to cover them. Season with salt and pepper, add a teaspoon of ground pimiento, cover the casserole, bring to the boil and simmer for 20 minutes. Remove the lid, add the drained clams, increase the heat and cook for a further 10 minutes. Serve the *caldeirada* – a true all-in-one dish – with boiled potatoes, or slices of toasted bread, or even polenta (like that used in the recipe for *Carne em vinha-d'alhos com milho frito*, pages 92-93).

Mixed white-flesh fish
   (frog fish, conger-eel, smooth-
   hound, turbot, skate, etc.),
   1.5 Kg; 2 lb 4 oz
Large clams, 500 g; 1 lb 2 oz
Squids (or cuttlefish), 600 g;
   1 1/4 lb
2 onions
3 cloves of garlic
3-4 ripe cooking tomatoes
Parsley
Piri-piri (see Explanations)
Ground pimiento
   (see Explanations)
Dry white wine
Boiled potatoes
   (for accompaniment)
Salt and pepper
Olive oil

Serves:	6-8
Preparation:	25'
Cooking:	45'
Difficulty:	● ●
Flavour:	● ● ●
Kcal (per serving):	384
Proteins (per serving):	44
Fats (per serving):	17
Nutritional value:	● ●

CAVALAS COM MOLHO DE VILÃO

Marinated mackerel with 'polenta' ☞ *Madeira*

4 single-portion mackerel,
   total approx. 1 Kg; 2 1/4 lb
6 cloves of garlic
Oregano, parsley, thyme
Piri-piri (see Explanations)
Dry white wine
White wine vinegar
Milho cozido (for serving,
   see end of Step 2)
Green leaf salad (for serving)
Salt and pepper
Olive oil

Serves: 4	
Preparation: 20'+5h	
Cooking: 15'	
Difficulty: ●●	
Flavour: ●●●	
Kcal (per serving): 479	
Proteins (per serving): 32	
Fats (per serving): 32	
Nutritional value: ●●	

1 Prepare the mackerel: slit the bellies open, remove the entrails, and rinse under running water. Season them inside and out with salt and pepper; put them in a large, wide bowl with the peeled and sliced garlic, a pinch of oregano, a few sprigs of thyme, a chopped sprig of parsley, the *piri-piri* crumbled and without its seeds, a cup of white wine and half a glass of vinegar. Leave to marinate for 4-5 hours, turning the fish over every now and then.

2 Thereafter, remove and drain the mackerel (keeping the marinade), dry them and fry them on both sides in a pan with a glass of hot oil (do not allow the oil to 'smoke'); remove and leave to drain on kitchen paper, keeping them in a warm place.

Pound the solid ingredients of the marinade in a mortar (or blender) and dilute the resulting paste with a little of the marinade liquid. Pour this mixture into the oil left in the pan and bring to the boil; allow the sauce to reduce and adjust for salt. Arrange the fried mackerel over a bed of green leaf salad on a platter and serve with the sauce and *milho cozido* (see recipe for *Carne em vinha-d'alhos com milho frito*, pages 92-93 Step 2; this takes about one hour to prepare and if included with the meal must be added to the total time required for this mackerel recipe).

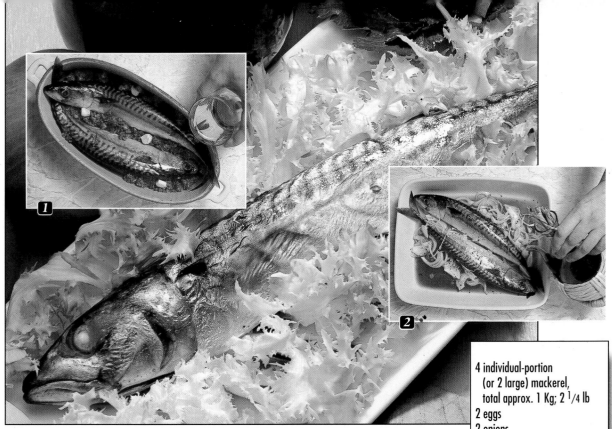

CAVALAS RECHEADAS

Stuffed mackerel ☞ *Azores*

1 Prepare the mackerel: slit them open, remove the entrails, rinse well inside and out and dry. Marinate them for 3 hours in a bowl with 2 glasses of wine, the crumbled *chouriço*, and 3 peeled and crushed cloves of garlic, turning them over every now and then. In the meantime, soak the bread in a small quantity of vinegar. Remove and drain the mackerel but keep the marinade. Hard-boil the eggs for 7 minutes after bringing the water to the boil; leave to cool for a few minutes then shell. Peel and finely chop the onions together with two cloves of garlic; sauté in a casserole with one tablespoon of melted cooking fat and 2-3 tablespoons of oil. Add the bread (squeezed of vinegar), the pitted and chopped olives, a chopped sprig of parsley and a pinch each of salt and pepper; mix and briefly blend the flavours.

2 Remove the casserole from the stove, transfer the contents into a bowl and mix with the chopped boiled eggs and the juice of the lemon. Allow this stuffing to cool then use it to fill the mackerel; sew the edges to avoid the stuffing escaping during cooking. Grease an ovenproof dish with cooking fat and arrange the mackerel on the bottom; cover with the remaining onion and clove of garlic (thinly sliced) and a finely chopped sprig of parsley; pour the marinade liquid and a teaspoon of tomato paste diluted with a little water over the ingredients, drizzle with oil and bake in the oven preheated to 180°C (350°F) for 20 minutes. Serve the mackerel with fresh green salad.

4 individual-portion (or 2 large) mackerel, total approx. 1 Kg; 2 ^{1}/$_4$ lb
2 eggs
2 onions
7 cloves of garlic
Hot *chouriço* (see Explanations), 50 g; 2 oz
10 black olives in brine
Tomato concentrate
1 slice of crustless bread
1 lemon
Parsley
Red wine vinegar
Dry white wine
Green leaf salad (for accompaniment)
Salt and pepper
Cooking fat, 30 g; 1 oz; 2 tbsp
Olive oil

Serves:	4
Preparation:	30'+3h
Cooking:	30'
Difficulty:	● ● ●
Flavour:	● ● ●
Kcal (per serving):	698
Proteins (per serving):	40
Fats (per serving):	45
Nutritional value:	● ● ●

CALDEIRADA DE ENGUIAS

Eel stew ☞ *Beira Litoral*

Medium sized eels, 1 Kg
Lard (thinly sliced), 100 g
6 medium-sized potatoes
3 onions
2 cloves of garlic
Bay leaf, mint and parsley
Saffron
Red wine vinegar
Salt (coarse and fine)
  and pepper
Olive oil

Serves: 6	
Preparation: 20'	
Cooking: 30'	
Difficulty: ● ●	
Flavour: ● ● ●	
Kcal (per serving): 992	
Proteins (per serving): 40	
Fats (per serving): 73	
Nutritional value: ● ● ●	

1 Prepare the eels by removing the heads, fins and entrails; rinse them well then dry. Skin them only if large eels are being used, otherwise just cut them into even-sized pieces. Peel and thinly slice the onions. Peel the potatoes and cut them into rounds. Put a layer of onions and one of potatoes at the bottom of an oiled, earthenware casserole (with a lid) then arrange a few pieces of eel over them.

2 Continue alternating these layers until all the ingredients have been used up (the eels must be on the top layer), remembering to season each layer with a drop of oil, a little chopped garlic, a few pieces torn off the bay leaf, small sprigs of parsley, a small pinch of saffron, and one each of salt and pepper. Arrange the slices of lard over the top of the *caldeirada*, so that all slices overlap; add a full glass of water, put the lid on the casserole, bring to the boil and simmer for 30 minutes.

3 Thereafter, take the lid off the casserole, remove the slices of lard and pound them in a mortar (or blender) with a teaspoon of coarse salt. Dilute this paste with 2 tablespoons of vinegar and a couple of tablespoons of the *caldeirada* cooking liquid; pour this sauce (called *moira*) over the *caldeirada* and serve garnished with sprigs of fresh mint.

*A boat
on the Ria de Aveiro.*

1

2

3

FATAÇA NA TELHA

Brick-baked grey-mullet ☞*Ribatejo*

1 deep-sea grey (or striped)
  mullet, approx. 1.2 Kg;
  2 ¹/₂ lb
Lard (fairly thick slices),
  200 g; 8 oz
1 large onion
Ground pimiento
  (see Explanations)
1 lemon
Parsley
Salt and freshly ground pepper
Olive oil

Serves: 4	
Preparation: 20'+1h	
Cooking: 30'	
Difficulty: ●	
Flavour: ● ● ●	
Kcal (per serving): 848	
Proteins (per serving): 38	
Fats (per serving): 74	
Nutritional value: ● ● ●	

This method of cooking originally foresaw the fish being put between two, tightly bound brick roof tiles (telhas) which were then placed in the glowing coals of a fire or in an open oven kindled by wood. However, unless you're willing to dismantle your rooftop, we suggest you use the specific brickware dish that can be found in shops selling kitchen equipment. Besides using grey mullet for this recipe, the Portuguese also bake savél (shad in English) in the telha, but since this is not always available at the fishmonger's, we think you'll enjoy the mullet.

Prepare the grey mullet: remove the scales, trim the fins, slit the belly open, remove the entrails and rinse well under cold running water. Season it inside and out with salt and pepper then leave to one side. Peel and chop the onion, then pound it to a paste in a mortar (or blender) with a sprig of parsley and a heaped teaspoon of ground pimiento. Spread this paste all over the fish, inside and out, and leave for one hour. Arrange a few slices of lard, not too near each other, at the bottom of a special brick-cooker (or crock-cooker) with a lid; place the fish over the lard, then add the remaining slices of lard, with spaces in between them as before. Put the lid on the brick-cooker and put it in the oven, pre-heated to 200°C (375-400°F), for 30'. When ready, remove the lid and drizzle the fish with a mixture of oil, lemon juice and freshly ground pepper.

This is the original recipe, in a simplified version; frozen lobsters instead of fresh ones may be used, or even scampi or prawns are just as delicious.

LAGOSTA À MODA DE PENICHE

Stewed lobster ☛ *Estremadura*

1 Peel and finely chop the onions; rinse the tomatoes, remove stalks, seeds and fibrous parts and slice. Peel and thinly slice the garlic, and rinse and dry a sprig of parsley then finely chop it. Remove the shell from the lobster and all traces of entrails; rinse, dry, then cut the flesh into slices 1 cm thick (approx. half an inch). Oil the bottom of a casserole (preferably earthenware with a lid) and cover it with a layer of the chopped garlic, parsley and onion, using half of the ingredients. Place half of the lobster slices over these ingredients and season with a pinch of ground pimiento and one each of salt and pepper.

2 Thereafter, put the tomato slices in a flat, compact layer, then the remaining slices of lobster. Cover with the remaining chopped garlic, parsley and onion, then the fresh pimientos (without seeds and in tiny pieces), one or two bay leaves, another pinch of salt and pepper, and one of ground pimiento. Pour a glass of wine over the ingredients, put the lid on the casserole and simmer over low heat for 45 minutes (or cook in the oven for about one hour at 150°C (310°F), then add a little more wine and cook for a further 20 minutes). Serve with boiled long-grain rice.

1 lobster (or crawfish) ready for use, approx. 1.2 Kg ; 2 1/2 lb
4 ripe cooking tomatoes
2 onions
2 cloves of garlic
2 fresh red pimiento
Bay leaf and parsley
Ground pimiento
Dry white wine
Boiled rice (for accompaniment)
Salt and pepper
Olive oil

Serves:	4
Preparation:	20′
Cooking:	45′
Difficulty:	●
Flavour:	● ● ●
Kcal (per serving):	588
Proteins (per serving):	50
Fats (per serving):	14
Nutritional value:	● ●

LULAS RECHEADAS

Stuffed squid ☞ *Algarve*

Medium-small squid,
  approx. 1 Kg; 2 1/4 lb
Lean cured ham (prosciutto),
  120 g; 5 oz
2 onions
5 ripe cooking tomatoes
2 cloves of garlic
1 egg
Bay leaf and parsley
Salt and pepper
Olive oil

Serves: 4	
Preparation: 25'	
Cooking: 40'	
Difficulty:	● ●
Flavour:	● ●
Kcal (per serving): 456	
Proteins (per serving): 36	
Fats (per serving): 30	
Nutritional value:	● ●

Peel the garlic and onions and rinse the tomatoes, removing their seeds. Prepare the squids: eliminate the 'tooth', eyes, entrails and cartilage, rinse, then separate the sac from the tentacles, which must be chopped together with the ham, one of the onions and one clove of garlic. Break the egg into the mixture and blend. Stuff the squids with the mixture and close them with a toothpick.

Finely chop the remaining onion and garlic, sauté in a casserole with 5-6 tablespoons of oil, and then add the tomatoes in pieces, a bay leaf and a chopped sprig of parsley. Add salt and pepper to taste, simmer for about ten minutes, then gently lower the squids into the sauce; cover and simmer for about 30 minutes, adding a little water whenever necessary to keep the squids soft and moist. Serve hot, sprinkled with chopped parsley.

PARGO NO FORNO

Oven-baked schnapper ☞ *Estremadura*

Clean the fish: remove the scales, slit the belly open and remove the entrails, rinse the fish in cold running water, then dry it. Peel the garlic and onion and finely chop. Rinse the tomatoes, remove stalks and seeds and cut into slices. Using half of the slices of tomato, cover the bottom of an ovenproof dish greased with oil; sprinkle with half of the chopped garlic and onion, plus 4-5 coriander seeds crushed in a mortar. Season the fish inside and out with salt and pepper then put it on top of these layers; cover with the remaining slices of tomato, chopped garlic and onion, and a further 4-5 crushed coriander seeds. Pour a glass of wine into the dish without allowing it to touch the fish, then put in the oven, preheated to 180°C (350°F), for 35 minutes, basting the fish every now and then with its sauce. Take the dish out of the oven, remove the fish and place it over a bed of sliced boiled potatoes on a platter; keep in a warm place. Put the ovenproof dish over low heat on the stove to reduce the sauce, crushing the tomatoes to a pulp with the back of a wooden spoon; sprinkle chopped parsley over the fish and serve it with its sauce.

1 schnapper (or dentex or
  sea bream), approx. 1 Kg;
  2 $^1/_4$ lb
5-6 ripe cooking tomatoes
1 onion
1 clove of garlic
Coriander seeds
Parsley (for garnish)
Boiled potatoes (for serving)
Dry white wine
Salt and pepper
Olive oil

Serves:	4
Preparation:	20'
Cooking:	40'
Difficulty:	●●
Flavour:	●●
Kcal (per serving):	544
Proteins (per serving):	44
Fats (per serving):	19
Nutritional value:	●●

POLVO GUISADO

Octopus in red wine ☞ *Azores*

Octopus (medium-small),
  approx. total 1.2 Kg; 2 lb
2 onions, 2 cloves of garlic
Bay leaf and parsley
Massa de pimentão
  (see opposite page)
Jamaica peppercorns
  (see opposite page)
Red wine
Boiled potatoes tossed in chopped
  parsley (for accompaniment)
Salt and peppercorns
Cooking fat, 35 g; 1 ¹/2 oz;
  2 ¹/4 bsp

Serves:	4
Preparation:	20′
Cooking:	1h
Difficulty:	● ●
Flavour:	● ●
Kcal (per serving):	460
Proteins (per serving):	32
Fats (per serving):	12
Nutritional value:	● ●

1 This method of cooking octopus is rather unique. Prepare the octopus by eliminating the entrails, eyes and 'tooth'; rinse it well under cold running water; dry it then cut it into rather small pieces. Melt the cooking fat (do not allow to 'smoke') in a casserole (preferably earthenware with a lid) and slowly sauté the peeled and chopped onions and cloves of garlic. When the onions are transparent, add the octopus, put the lid on the casserole and simmer very, very slowly over the lowest heat possible to 'sweat out' the liquid contained in the octopus flesh.

2 Gradually remove all the moisture released with a ladle and keep to one side, continuing to simmer (with lid on and over minimum heat) until all the pieces of octopus are almost dry.

3 At this point, add some of the octopus liquid together with 4-5 peppercorns, 7-8 Jamaica peppercorns, a heaped teaspoon of *massa de pimentão* and a pinch of salt, and a bay leaf; when the octopus has absorbed this liquid, add some more, continuing to do so (putting the lid back on between one addition of liquid and another) until all the octopus liquid has been used up.

4 Very gradually add 2 full glasses of wine, allowing the octopus to absorb it in the same way as the liquid in Step 3, covering the casserole after every addition of wine. When all the wine has been poured in, leave the casserole uncovered to reduce the sauce. Serve the octopus with its thick sauce and boiled potatoes tossed in chopped parsley.

Massa de pimentão *is a paste made from the typical pimientos that* grow in the Azores: *red, triangular in shape and more or less hot,* their stalks and seeds are removed after they are split open, then they are made into a paste with coarse salt in a mortar. If this massa *is difficult to find it may be substituted with the pimiento* paste that is sold in tubes. Jamaica pepper (or pimiento) *is the dried* berries of a plant belonging to the myrtle family originally from Central America: it has a distinct fragrance, with a hint of cinnamon, clove and nutmeg.

RAIA COM MOLHO DE PITAU

Skate in savoury sauce ☞ *Beira Litoral*

Skate fillets, 700 g; 1 ¹/₂ lb
6 medium-sized potatoes
2 cloves of garlic
1 salted anchovy
Bay leaf
Ground pimiento
  (see Explanations)
Vinegar
Salt and pepper
Olive oil

Serves: 4	
Preparation: 15'+1h	
Cooking: 30'	
Difficulty: ●	
Flavour: ● ● ●	
Kcal (per serving): 550	
Proteins (per serving): 46	
Fats (per serving): 31	
Nutritional value: ● ●	

Sprinkle a little salt over the skate fillets, lay them flat on a platter and leave them for about one hour. In the meantime, boil the potatoes in slightly salted water and when cooked peel them and keep them in a warm place. Take the skate fillets from the platter and blanch them for 10 minutes in unsalted water, leaving them to cool in their cooking liquid.

To make the sauce, heat half a glass of oil in a small pot and very slowly sauté the peeled garlic crushed with a bay leaf, a teaspoonful of ground pimiento and a pinch of pepper in it, but do not allow the garlic to brown. Rinse and fillet the anchovy and add it to the sauce, with a drop of vinegar, allowing it to disintegrate slowly; let the flavours mix a few minutes but do not allow to boil.

Cut both the fish and the potatoes into fingers all the same size; place them alternately on a serving platter and pour the sauce over them. The original recipe calls for using the skate liver instead of a salted anchovy but, since this is not always easy to find, we have devised this alternative.

SARDINHAS ASSADAS

Grilled sardines ☛ *Estremadura*

Prepare the sardines by eliminating their entrails and rinsing them several times under cold running water; place them side by side on a platter and sprinkle a handful of coarse salt all over them; leave to one side for an hour. Rub them with a clean cloth to remove all traces of salt and, if wished, brush them with a little olive oil (they are much better without it, however). Grill them over dying embers or under the grill of the oven (five minutes each side). Serve immediately accompanied with a mixed salad (lettuce, sweet peppers, cucumber, tomatoes, etc.)

24-32 (depending on the size)
  very fresh sardines
Mixed fresh salad
  (for accompaniment)
Coarse sea salt
Olive oil (optional)

Serves: 4	
Preparation: 15'+1h	
Cooking: 10'	
Difficulty: ●	
Flavour: ● ● ●	
Kcal (per serving): 316	
Proteins (per serving): 30	
Fats (per serving): 20	
Nutritional value: ● ●	

TRUTA À MODA DE BARROSO

Trout with lard ☞ *Alto Douro*

4 single-portion rainbow
  or mountain trout, total 1 Kg;
  2 ¹/₄ lb
Lean smoked ham (thinly
  sliced), 60 g; 2 oz
Lard, 100 g (or 50 g of cooking
  fat); 4 oz; ¹/₂ cup
Lettuce or endive salad
  (for serving)
Salt and pepper

Serves: 4	
Preparation: 30'	
Cooking: 30'	
Difficulty: ● ●	
Flavour: ● ●	
Kcal (per serving): 655	
Proteins (per serving): 51	
Fats (per serving): 48	
Nutritional value: ● ● ●	

First of all, clean the trout: remove their scales and entrails then rinse them well under cold running water and dry them. Cut the slices of ham into strips, roll them up and tuck them into the trout bellies, together with a pinch each of salt and pepper.

Cut the lard (or cooking fat) into cubes and melt them slowly (do not fry) in a pan; cook the trout (one at a time, if necessary) in this, without allowing the fat to 'smoke' and turning the fish over when the first side is cooked. Serve them with a fresh green leaf salad dressed with the liquefied fat left in the pan.

TRUTAS ABAFADAS

Soused trout ☛ *Beira Alta*

4 single-portion rainbow or
 mountain trout, total 1 Kg;
 2 1/4 lb
3 cloves of garlic
Bay leaf and parsley
Nutmeg
White wine vinegar
Boiled potatoes tossed
 in chopped parsley
Salt and pepper
Olive oil

Serves: 4	
Preparation: 20'	
Cooking: 20'	
Difficulty: ● ●	
Flavour: ● ●	
Kcal (per serving): 570	
Proteins (per serving): 52	
Fats (per serving): 26	
Nutritional value: ●	

Prepare the trout: remove the scales, trim the fins, slit the bellies open to remove the entrails, rinse well inside and out. Peel and finely slice the cloves of garlic then sauté in a large pan with 4 table-spoons of oil and a bay leaf; when the garlic begins to colour, add 2 glasses of vinegar, a chopped sprig of parsley, a pinch of salt, a dash pepper and a little grated nutmeg. As soon as this marinade starts to boil, put the trout into it and cook them, first on one side for 7-8 minutes then on the other; transfer the trout to a deep dish and allow them to cool. Since these trout are to be eaten cold, they are even better the next day after cooking them; serve on a bed of lettuce and accompanied by boiled potatoes tossed in chopped parsley.

BACALHAU À ASSIS

Dried codfish with vegetables ☞ *Beira Baixa*

Dried codfish fish, pre-soaked,
  700 g; 1 ¹/₂ lb
3 eggs
Lean cured ham (prosciutto),
  100 g (4 oz), in one piece
4 medium-sized potatoes
3 carrots
1 onion
1 sweet pepper
Parsley
Olive oil

Serves: 4	
Preparation: 25'	
Cooking: 25'	
Difficulty: ● ●	
Flavour: ● ● ●	
Kcal (per serving): 603	
Proteins (per serving): 51	
Fats (per serving): 27	
Nutritional value: ● ● ●	

Rinse the cod well then remove the skin. Remove the stalk, seeds and fibrous parts of the sweet pepper. Peel the potatoes and scrape the skin off the carrots and blanch for 10 minutes in slightly salted boiling water; drain well then cut both types of vegetable into julienne strips. Peel and finely slice the onion and sauté in a casserole with 3-4 tablespoons of oil, the diced sweet pepper and cubed ham. When these vegetables are tender, add the cod cut into small pieces and cook until soft. A few moments before the cod is ready, add the julienne carrots and potatoes; mix to blend the flavours then remove from the stove. Add the beaten eggs and a finely chopped sprig of parsley; mix carefully then serve hot. No salt is added to this recipe because that in both the dried codfish and the ham is sufficient.

BACALHAU À BRÁS

Dried codfish with potatoes and onions ☛ *Estremadura*

1 Rinse the dried cod under cold running water, remove the skin and any bones and tough parts; flake the flesh. Peel the potatoes, rinse then slice into fingers or into matchstick chips using a chip-cutter. Deep-fry them till pale golden in hot frying oil; remove with a draining spoon and allow to dry on kitchen paper.

2 Peel and finely slice the onion; sauté with the peeled and finely chopped garlic in a casserole (preferably earthenware) with 4-5 tablespoons of olive oil. Add the cod flakes and simmer over minimum heat, mixing very carefully. Add the potatoes, then the eggs, beaten with a pinch each of salt and pepper; keeping the heat at minimum, mix all the ingredients very gently until a creamy consistency is achieved. Turn out the contents of the casserole onto a serving platter, sprinkle with chopped parsley and garnish with black olives.

Dried codfish, pre-soaked, 700 g; 1 1/2 lb	
4 eggs	
4 potatoes	
1 onion	
1 clove of garlic	
Parsley	
Black olives (for accompaniment)	
Salt and pepper	
Frying oil	
Olive oil	

Serves:	4
Preparation:	20'
Cooking:	25'
Difficulty:	●●
Flavour:	●●●
Kcal (per serving):	730
Proteins (per serving):	52
Fats (per serving):	41
Nutritional value:	●●●

BACALHAU À GOMES DE SÁ

Dried codfish cooked with milk and potatoes ☞ *Douro*

Dried codfish, pre-soaked,
   800 g; 1 3/4 lb
5 medium-sized potatoes
2 eggs
1 onion
1 clove of garlic
24 pitted black olives in brine
Full milk, 0.5 litres; 3/4 pint
Salt and pepper
Olive oil

Serves: 4	
Preparation: 20'+2h 20'	
Cooking: 40'	
Difficulty: ●●	
Flavour: ●●●	
Kcal (per serving): 499	
Proteins (per serving): 54	
Fats (per serving): 25	
Nutritional value: ●●	

1 Rinse the dried cod well under cold running water, dry it then put it into a large casserole (or ovenproof dish) with a lid; cover with boiling water, put the lid on the casserole and leave for 20 minutes.

2 Drain the cod, remove the skin, bones and tough parts and cut into small even-sized pieces; put these back into the casserole (after throwing away the liquid) and cover with boiling milk. Put the lid back on and leave to stand for a couple of hours. In the meantime, rinse the potatoes, boil them then peel them while still hot; keep to one side. Hard-boil the eggs for 7 minutes after the water starts to boil; allow them to cool then shell them; keep these to one side as well.

3 Peel and finely slice the onion and the clove of garlic and slowly sauté until golden in a casserole with half a glass of oil; add the sliced potatoes and the well-drained cod, a pinch of salt (this is required since the cod has soaked in milk) and a pinch of pepper. Re-heat all the ingredients over minimum heat but do not allow to boil; stir very gently to blend all the flavours.

4 Distribute the contents of the casserole in layers in an ovenproof dish, alternating the layers of cod with layers of potatoes, pour the oil left in the casserole over the ingredients then bake in the oven, preheated to 220°C (410-459°F), for 10 minutes. Serve sprinkled with chopped parsley and garnished with slices of boiled egg and the black olives.

BACALHAU À LAGAREIRO

Oven-baked, marinated dried codfish ☞ *Douro e Minho*

Dried codfish, pre-soaked,
  800 g; 1 3/4 lb
4 cloves of garlic
2 eggs,1 lemon
Fine, dry breadcrumbs,
  40 g; 2 oz; 4 tbsp
Full milk, 0.5 litres; 3/4 pint
Green-leaf salad
  (for accompaniment)
Salt and pepper, olive oil

Serves: 4	
Preparation: 20'+2h	
Cooking: 25'	
Difficulty: ● ●	
Flavour: ● ● ●	
Kcal (per serving): 479	
Proteins (per serving): 54	
Fats (per serving): 21	
Nutritional value: ● ●	

1 Rinse the dried cod under cold running water, remove the skin and cut the flesh into even-sized pieces; put these in a bowl with the peeled and sliced garlic, a pinch each of salt and pepper, the juice of the lemon, and cover with the milk. Leave to marinate for two hours then remove and drain the pieces of cod (keep the liquid).

2 Dip the pieces of cod into the beaten eggs, leave them there for a few minutes, then dip them in the breadcrumbs until evenly coated; pour 6 tablespoons of oil and 3-4 tablespoons of the marinade into an ovenproof dish; arrange the cod pieces side by side in the dish and bake in the oven for 25 minutes at 180°C (350°F); during this time, add more marinade whenever necessary to avoid the cod drying out. Serve accompanied by a green-leaf salad (or boiled potatoes tossed in chopped parsley).

70

BACALHAU ASSADO COM BATATAS A MURRO

Grilled dried codfish with potatoes ☛ *Beira Alta*

Rinse the dried cod under cold running water, dry it and remove the skin, bones and tough parts; cut into even-sized pieces and grill over glowing (but not kindling) embers, or under the grill of the oven, for 4 minutes on each side. Using an earthenware or copper casserole, slowly heat (but do not allow to boil) a glass of oil with the peeled and crushed cloves of garlic and a pinch of pepper; remove from the heat, transfer the contents of the casserole into a bowl, add the pieces of cod and leave to absorb the flavours for about twenty minutes. Rinse the potatoes well (do not peel), toss them in coarse salt in a bowl, put them in an ovenproof dish and bake them in the oven, preheated to 180°C (350°F), for 20 minutes. Halfway through the cooking time, remove them from the oven, press them with the palm of your hand (be careful – they'll be really hot!) so that they split in the middle (but do not squash them) then put them back into the oven, sprinkle more coarse salt over them and finish cooking. Serve the grilled cod with these simply delicious potatoes.

Dried codfish, pre-soaked, 800 g; 1 3/4 lb
12 small potatoes
4-5 cloves of garlic
Coarse salt, pepper
Olive oil

Serves:	4
Preparation:	20'+20'
Cooking:	20'
Difficulty:	● ●
Flavour:	● ● ●
Kcal (per serving):	510
Proteins (per serving):	50
Fats (per serving):	13
Nutritional value:	● ●

BACALHAU ASSADO COM BROA

Crispy oven-baked dried codfish ☞ *Beira Litoral*

Dried codfish, pre-soaked,
   800 g; 1 ³/₄ lb
4 crustless slices of *broa*
   (see Step 1)
1 onion
3 cloves of garlic, bay leaf
Ground pimiento
   (see Explanations)
Dry white wine
Mixed salad
   (for accompaniment)
Ground pepper and peppercorns
Cooking fat, 20 g; 1 ¹/₂ oz;
   1 ¹/₂ tbsp
Olive oil

Serves: 4	
Preparation: 15′	
Cooking: 25′	
Difficulty: ●●	
Flavour: ●●●	
Kcal (per serving): 573	
Proteins (per serving): 49	
Fats (per serving): 17	
Nutritional value: ●●●	

1 Rinsed the dried cod, remove the skin and cut the flesh into even-sized pieces; put these into an oven-proof dish (greased well with oil) and add a glass of wine, a bay leaf and 3-4 peppercorns. Put in the oven, preheated to 200°C (375-400°F), and cook for 10 minutes. In the meantime, sprinkle a generous amount of wine over the slices of *broa* (see recipe for *Migas da Lousã* at page 34 Steps 1 and 2) in a bowl, crumble them and mix them with the peeled and finely chopped onion and garlic; melt the cooking fat and pour it over the mixture, add a pinch of ground pepper, mix thoroughly then leave to one side for a few minutes.

2 Remove the dish from the oven, spread the *broa* mixture over the pieces of cod, and then put the dish back into the oven until the pieces of cod are golden-brown and crisp. Serve with fried potatoes or mixed salad.

BACALHAU PODRE

Fried dried codfish with potatoes ☞ *Alto Douro*

1 Rinse the dried cod well, remove the skin then cut the fish into four fillets; put these in a pan, cover with cold water and put on the stove. When the water starts to boil, remove the fillets with a draining spoon (keep the cooking liquid). Beat one of the eggs with the flour, gradually adding enough cold water to make a soft batter. Dip the cod fillets into the batter, coat them well and fry them in a pan with 4-5 tablespoons of olive oil, making sure they are golden crisp on both sides. Remove them from the oil with a draining spoon and leave them to dry on kitchen paper. Peel the potatoes, cut them into rounds (not too thin) and toss-fry them with a little salt in the oil left in the pan.

2 Peel the onion and cut it into slices, peel and crush the clove of garlic; sauté these in a large ovenproof dish (preferably earthenware with a lid) with a bay leaf, 2-3 tablespoons of oil and 4-5 tablespoons of the cod cooking liquid. When the onion is tender, remove the dish from the stove, arrange half the potato rounds in a layer over the onion, then the cod fillets; lastly make another layer with the remaining potatoes and sprinkle with chopped parsley. Beat the remaining eggs and a pinch each of salt and pepper with an egg whisk (or hand mixer) until they are soft and fluffy; pour this over the cod and potatoes. Put the lid back on the dish and bake in a slow oven (140°C; 300°F) for 10-12 minutes, until the egg mixture is cooked. Serve sprinkled with chopped parsley.

Dried codfish, pre-soaked, 700 g; 1 lb 10 oz
5 eggs
8 medium-sized potatoes
1 onion
1 clove of garlic
Bay leaf and parsley
Plain flour, 20 g; 1 ¹/2 oz; 1 ¹/2 tbsp
Salt and pepper, olive oil

Serves:	4
Preparation:	20'
Cooking:	25'
Difficulty:	●●
Flavour:	●●●
Kcal (per serving):	721
Proteins (per serving):	58
Fats (per serving):	25
Nutritional value:	●●●

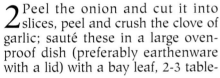

BOLA DE BACALHAU

Dried codfish pie *Trás-os-Montes*

Dried codfish, pre-soaked,
  800 g; 1 ³/4 lb
Plain flour, 400 g; 12 oz-1 lb
3 onions, 2 cloves of garlic
Baker's yeast, 15 g; ¹/2 oz;
  1 tbsp
Cooking fat, 20 g; ³/4 oz;
  1 ¹/2 tbsp , olive oil

Serves: 4	
Preparation: 35'÷2h	
Cooking: 35'	
Difficulty: ● ● ●	
Flavour: ● ● ●	
Kcal (per serving): 716	
Proteins (per serving): 54	
Fats (per serving): 18	
Nutritional value: ● ● ●	

1 Sift the flour into a mixing bowl, dilute the yeast with a little luke-warm water and put it into a well in the centre of the flour. Work the dough with the appropriate beaters on a hand mixer, incorporating the cooking fat and sufficient water to make a smooth, stiff dough. Cover the bowl with a clean cloth and leave to rise for a couple of hours.

2 In the meantime, peel and finely slice the onions and garlic and sauté them (do not allow to colour) in a casserole with 7-8 tablespoons of oil. Rinse the dried cod, remove the skin and any bones or tough parts and flake the flesh; add these flakes to the casserole and simmer for about ten minutes.

3 Uncover the dough, knead it for a short while by hand, roll it out and divide it into two unequal parts (about ²/3 and ¹/3); using the larger of the two pieces, line an oil-greased, ovenproof dish (or pie dish, as long as it not too deep but can hold the filling).

4 Fill the pastry-case in the dish with the cod and its sauce, smooth out the surface, then cover with the other piece of pastry and seal the edges. Use pastry trimmings to decorate the top of the pie and brush the top with beaten egg. Bake in the oven, preheated to 200°C (375-400°F), for about 20 minutes.

3

4

PASTÉIS DE BACALHAU

Dried codfish and potato croquettes ☛ *Minho*

Dried codfish, pre-soaked,
 400 g; 12 oz-1 lb
5 medium-sized potatoes
4 eggs
1 onion
Parsley
Nutmeg
Dry white wine
2-3 lemons, lettuce
 (for garnish)
Salt and pepper
Frying oil

Serves: 4	
Preparation: 25'	
Cooking: 40'	
Difficulty: ● ● ●	
Flavour: ● ●	
Kcal (per serving): 695	
Proteins (per serving): 38	
Fats (per serving): 36	
Nutritional value: ● ● ●	

Rinse the cod well, remove the skin and any bones or tough parts; cut into fillets and put them in a pan, covering them with cold water. Bring to the boil and immediately remove and drain the fillets. Rinse the potatoes, boil them then peel them while still hot; mash them with a potato-masher (or put them in a mixer) and put the mashed potatoes into a bowl. Mix the finely flaked cod into the potatoes, together with the peeled onion chopped with a sprig of parsley, a pinch of grated nutmeg, a tiny pinch of salt and a pinch of pepper. Pour in half a glass of wine and the well-beaten eggs; gently mix all the ingredients by hand or with a hand-mixer to obtain a smooth, stiff consistency. Divide the mixture into balls and shape them into croquettes (*quenelles* in French; rissoles in many English-speaking countries) and fry them in plenty of hot oil. Serve them decorated with sprigs of parsley over a bed of lettuce and surrounded by wedges of lemon.

Meat and POULTRY

*Delicious smells are about to waft out of this
section: besides simple, quickly prepared
dishes that are nevertheless very tempting,
there is a series of more elaborate recipes,
what one might call culinary masterpieces,
both hearty and sophisticated, to be served
on special occasions (don't worry, these
recipes only look difficult to do, but they are
not), like Cozido, Rojões com belouras
or the great Peru recheado.
The meat in these dishes is often marinated
and on many occasions is accompanied
by vegetables, croquettes or even seafood,
like in the exquisite and unusual
Lombo de porco com amêijoas.*

4

BIFES DE CEBOLADA

Braised beef and onions ☞ *Estremadura*

4 slices (or rib steaks) of beef,
    total 600 g; 1 lb 6 oz
3 onions
2-3 ripe cooking tomatoes
2 cloves of garlic
Bay leaf
Parsley
French-fried potatoes
    (for accompaniment)
Salt and pepper
Olive oil

Serves: 4	
Preparation: 15'	
Cooking: 30'	
Difficulty: ●	
Flavour: ●●	
Kcal (per serving): 363	
Proteins (per serving): 35	
Fats (per serving): 12	
Nutritional value: ●	

Rinse the tomatoes, remove stalks and seeds then slice. Peel and finely slice the onions; arrange them over the bottom of a casserole (preferably earthenware with a lid), drizzle with a little oil, then place the meat on top of them. Cover the meat with the slices of tomato, adding the peeled and sliced garlic and chopped parsley. Between one layer and another, season with a little salt and pepper and add tiny pieces torn off a bay leaf. Put the lid on the casserole and cook slowly for about 30 minutes; if the gravy appears to be too thin, reduce it by taking the lid off the casserole for the last five minutes. Serve the meat with its sauce and French-fried potatoes.

VITELA ASSADA

Rump steak in salt ☛ *Beira Alta*

Beef loin or rump steak
(a nice firm cut), 800 g;
1 ³/₄ lb
Mixed salad and spring onions
(for serving)
Coarse salt and pepper

Serves:	4
Preparation:	10'
Cooking:	40'
Difficulty:	●
Flavour:	● ●
Kcal (per serving):	179
Proteins (per serving):	40
Fats (per serving):	2
Nutritional value:	●

This is another simple, yet delicious dish. Bind the cut of meat with kitchen string to keep it together (it will probably be necessary); moisten it with a little water all over and put it into a dish containing a thick layer of coarse salt. Turn it over and over in the salt until it is thoroughly coated, then pierce it right through with the type of skewer required for traditional spit-roasting over an open fire (this also calls for placing a dripping-pan underneath it to collect the gravy). If no open fire is available, the roasting-jack in an ordinary oven may be used (temperature at 180°C; 350°F for 40 minutes) or even just an ovenproof dish with a lid (preferably earthenware), or a crock-roaster, with the oven at 200°C (375-400°F). When the meat is ready, remove it from the heat, unwind the string and draw out the skewer; scrape off as much salt as possible and serve it with a mixed salad and spring onions.

CABRITO ASSADO

Oven-roasted saddle of kid ☛ *Ribatejo*

Saddle of kid, approx. 1.4 Kg; 3 lb
Chouriço de carne (see Explanations), 100 g; 4 oz
Lard (one piece), 80 g; 3 oz
1 onion
2 cloves of garlic
1 dry red pimiento
Mild ground pimiento (see Explanations)
Parsley
Dry white wine
New potatoes (for accompaniment), 500 g; 1 lb 2 oz
Salt
Olive oil

Serves:	4
Preparation:	20'+6h
Cooking:	1h 10'
Difficulty:	● ●
Flavour:	● ● ●
Kcal (per serving):	763
Proteins (per serving):	49
Fats (per serving):	45
Nutritional value:	● ● ●

1 Peel the onion and cut it into wedges; blend it in a mixer with the peeled garlic, the dry pimiento without its seeds, the *chouriço*, the lard and a sprig of parsley. Put this mixture into a bowl, add a teaspoonful of ground pimiento and a pinch of salt, then dilute it with half a glass of wine. Mix well.

2 Spread this mixture all over the saddle of kid (tied with string to keep it together) so that it is evenly coated; place the kid on a platter, cover it with a food dome and leave it to absorb the flavours for 5-6 hours.

3 Remove the kid from the platter and put it into a large, oil-greased ovenproof dish; cook in the oven, preheated to 180°C (350°F), for 45 minutes, basting it every now and then with its own gravy, or with a little hot water if the gravy is insufficient.

4 Remove the dish from the oven, arrange the brushed, rinsed and dried potatoes (with their skins left on) all around the meat, turn them over and over until they are coated with the gravy, and sprinkle with a little salt. Put the dish back into the oven and cook for a further 25 minutes; when ready, unwind the string around the meat and serve with the roast potatoes.

The Casa dos Patudos, at Alpiarça.

PERNA DE BORREGO NO TACHO

Leg of lamb in garlic ☛ *Algarve*

One leg of lamb (or kid),
   approx. 1 Kg; 2 1/4 lb
6 medium-sized potatoes
1 whole head of garlic
Bay leaf, parsley
Mild ground pimiento
   (see Explanations)
1 clove
Tomato purée
Red wine vinegar
Dry white wine
Tomato and cucumber salad
   (for accompaniment)
Salt, peppercorns
Cooking fat, 50 g; 2 oz; 5 tbsp

Serves:	4
Preparation:	15'+4h
Cooking:	1h 15'
Difficulty:	● ●
Flavour:	● ● ●
Kcal (per serving):	596
Proteins (per serving):	47
Fats (per serving):	17
Nutritional value:	● ●

1 Pound the peeled garlic in a mortar (or mixer) with a pinch of salt; spread this paste all over the leg of lamb and put the meat in a deep casserole (preferably earthenware) with a lid and leave it to absorb the flavours for one hour. Thereafter, pour a full glass of wine and half a glass of vinegar (diluted with a little water) over the lamb; sprinkle evenly over the surface the leaves from a sprig of parsley, a bay leaf, a teaspoonful of ground pimiento, 4-5 peppercorns, 3-4 tablespoons of tomato purée and pieces of cooking fat. Leave to stand for 3 hours, turning the meat over every now and then.

2 Put the lid on the casserole, place it on the stove and bring to the boil slowly; simmer for just under one hour then add the peeled potatoes cut into chunks and taste for salt; put the lid back on and cook until the potatoes are ready. Serve the leg of lamb with a tomato and cucumber salad – and this becomes an all-in-one meal.

COELHO À CAÇADORA

Game-hunter's rabbit ☞ *Estremadura*

1 rabbit (ready for use), approx. 1.3 Kg; 2 3/4 lb
2 medium-sized onions
Thinly sliced smoked bacon, 150 g; 6 oz
4 ripe cooking tomatoes
3 cloves of garlic
Bay leaf, parsley
Tomato concentrate (optional)
Red wine vinegar
Red wine
Salt and pepper
Cooking fat, 50 g; 1 1/2 oz; 5 tbsp

Serves: 4	
Preparation: 15'	
Cooking: 1h	
Difficulty:	● ●
Flavour:	● ● ●
Kcal (per serving): 880	
Proteins (per serving): 46	
Fats (per serving): 60	
Nutritional value:	● ● ●

Rinse the rabbit well and cut it into a dozen or so pieces (eliminate the head). Rinse the tomatoes, remove the stalks and seeds and cut into thin slices. Peel and finely slice the onions; grease a casserole (preferably earthenware and with a lid) with the cooking fat and cover the bottom with the slices of onion. Put the rabbit pieces on top of the onions, season with salt and pepper, add the peeled and chopped garlic, the sliced tomatoes, the slices of smoked bacon, and sprinkle with chopped parsley. Put the lid on the casserole and simmer very slowly over minimum heat for just under one hour. Five minutes before the end of cooking, add a glass of wine mixed with 2-3 tablespoons of vinegar (if desired, a teaspoonful of tomato concentrate can be diluted in the wine and vinegar at this point). Raise the heat under the casserole, bring to the boil without the lid on and reduce the liquid; remove from the heat and serve.

COELHO DE CEBOLADA

Sweet and sour rabbit with onions ☞ *Trás-os-Montes*

1 rabbit (ready for use),
   approx. 1.3 Kg; 2 3/4 lb
4 medium-sized onions
Vegetable broth (made
   with bouillon cubes)
Sugar
Red wine vinegar
Salt and pepper
Olive oil

Serves: 4	
Preparation: 15′	
Cooking: 1h 20′	
Difficulty: ●●	
Flavour: ●●●	
Kcal (per serving): 507	
Proteins (per serving): 52	
Fats (per serving): 19	
Nutritional value: ●●	

1 Rinse and dry the rabbit, then cut it into a dozen or so pieces (eliminate the head). Peel and finely slice the onions, put them in an ovenproof dish (preferably earthenware with a lid) with 2-3 tablespoons of oil, a drop of broth and a pinch of salt; sauté very slowly without the lid on until the onions are transparent and soft. Sprinkle them with two tablespoons of sugar, raise the heat under the casserole and, stirring with care, caramelise the onions for about ten minutes, moistening them with a little broth if they become too dry.

2 Add the pieces of rabbit, turn them over so that they become coated with the onions, season with salt and pepper, pour 2-3 tablespoons of vinegar into the casserole and slowly brown the rabbit for about ten minutes. Put the lid on the casserole and cook in a preheated oven (160°C; 320°F)) for about one hour, until the rabbit is tender.

GALINHA CEREJADA

Hen casserole ☞ *Algarve*

1 Divide the hen in four (discard the head) and put it in a large casserole with the bacon, *linguiça* (or *chouriço*), one of the onions peeled and cut into wedges and a sprig of parsley. Cover with plenty of water and bring to the boil; put the lid on the casserole, lower the heat and simmer for 45 minutes. Remove the hen and cured meats from the broth, drain them well and keep to one side (the broth is to be kept). Peel and chop the other onion and sauté it slowly in a casserole (preferably earthenware) with 2-3 tablespoons of oil, the cooking fat, the peeled and finely sliced garlic and a sprig of parsley.

2 Cut the hen into a dozen or so pieces and brown them evenly all over in the casserole with the sautéed onion; add as glass of wine and a pinch of salt (very little) and cook for about 30 minutes over very low heat. In the meantime, boil the rice in the meat broth, taste for salt, then drain in a colander. Arrange the pieces of hen in a serving platter accompanied by the rice covered with strips of bacon and *linguiça* or *chouriço*.

Linguiça *is a sausage containing minced pork generously seasoned with ground pimiento.*

1 young boiling hen (ready for use), approx. 1.5 Kg;
  3 lb 6 oz
Soup rice, 300 g; 12 oz;
  1 2/3 cups
Unsmoked bacon (in 1 slice),
  120 g; 1/4 lb
Linguiça (see below Step 2)
  or *chouriço de carne*
  (see Explanations), 100 g; 4 oz
2 onions
2 cloves of garlic
Parsley
Dry white wine
Salt, olive oil
Cooking fat, 10 g; 1/2 oz; 1/2 tbsp

Serves: 6	
Preparation: 15′	
Cooking: 1h 20′	
Difficulty: ● ●	
Flavour: ● ● ●	
Kcal (per serving): 978	
Proteins (per serving): 39	
Fats (per serving): 63	
Nutritional value: ● ● ●	

EMPADAS DE GALINHA

Hen and sausage pies ☛ *Alentejo*

1 young boiling hen (ready for use), approx. 1.5 Kg; 3 lb
Plain flour, 500 g; 1 lb 2 oz; 4 cups
Smoked bacon (one slice), 250 g; 9 oz
1 *chouriço* (see Explanations) or *linguiça* (see page 85)
2 eggs
1 onion
2 cloves of garlic
Parsley, marjoram
2 cloves
Dry white wine
Red wine vinegar
Salt, peppercorns
Olive oil

Serves: 6	
Preparation: 50'	
Cooking: 1h 20'	
Difficulty: ● ● ●	
Flavour: ● ● ●	
Kcal (per serving): 1358	
Proteins (per serving): 60	
Fats (per serving): 76	
Nutritional value: ● ● ●	

1 A dozen 12 cm (5 inch) diameter pie tins will be needed for this recipe. Put the hen in a large pan with the bacon, the *chouriço*, the peeled and chopped onion and garlic, a sprig each of parsley and marjoram, the cloves and about 10 peppercorns. Cover these ingredients with slightly salted water mixed with two full glass of wine and 3-4 tablespoons of vinegar, bring to the boil, cover the pan, lower the heat to minimum and simmer at length, until the flesh on the hen starts to come away from the bones.

2 Remove the hen and the cured meats from the pan; filter and keep the broth (do not discard the fat parts left in the sieve). Carefully bone the hen and chop the meat, bacon and *chouriço* with a chopper (or food mixer).

3 Sift the flour into a bowl, add the fats left in the sieve, a little of the broth and mix all together with a hand mixer, adding more broth every now and then until the resulting dough is compact and smooth; make the dough into a ball and leave to stand for a few minutes.

4 Roll the dough out to 5 mm thick (³/4 inch) then, using the pie tins for size, cut out disks of pastry the right size for lining them; oil the tins and fit the pastry cases inside, pressing down with your fingertips. Knead the pastry trimmings, roll out again and cut out other disks, suitable in size for covering the *empadas* pastry cases previously made.

5 Spoon the meat mixture into the pastry cases, moisten with a little broth, then cover them with the pastry lids; moisten the edges and press together to seal. Brush the tops with beaten egg and put the *empadas* in the oven, preheated to 180°C (350°F), and bake until golden brown (about 20 minutes). Remove from the pie tins and serve hot.

Estremoz,
in the Alentejana plains.

FRANGO NA PÚCARA

Chicken in a crock-roaster ☛ *Estremadura*

1 chicken (ready for use),
approx. 1.2 Kg;
2 1/2-2 3/4 lb
Smoked raw ham (sliced),
100 g; 4 oz
12 round, baby onions
3 ripe cooking tomatoes
1 sweet pepper
2 cloves of garlic
Strong, ready-made mustard
Chopped parsley
Dry white wine
Brandy
Tawny port
Salt and pepper

Serves:	4
Preparation:	20'
Cooking:	1h 30'
Difficulty:	● ●
Flavour:	● ● ●
Kcal (per serving):	743
Proteins (per serving):	35
Fats (per serving):	40
Nutritional value:	● ● ●

The chicken must be already plucked, its entrails removed, singed over a flame to eliminate residual quills, rinsed and dried. Cut it into a dozen or so pieces. Trim and rinse the vegetables: cut the tomatoes into wedges and the pepper into strips. Line the bottom of a heavy, ovenproof dish with a lid (preferably an earthenware crock-roaster) with the slices of ham and arrange the pieces of chicken over these. Arrange all the vegetables (peeled onions, tomato wedges, strips of pepper, crushed garlic) around and over the chicken and season with salt and pepper; dilute a tablespoon of mustard paste in a glass and a half of wine and pour over the chicken and vegetables. Put the lid on the crock and put in the oven preheated to 180°C (350°F); cook for one hour and fifteen minutes. Remove the crock from the oven, uncover, and sprinkle the contents with a liqueur-glass of brandy and one of tawny port; put the crock back in the oven (without its lid) for a further 15 minutes. When ready, sprinkle the chicken with chopped parsley and serve.

ISCAS COM ELAS

Sliced liver with potatoes ☛ *Estremadura*

1

2

Pig's liver, 700 g; 1 ¹/₂ lb
4 cloves of garlic
Bay leaf and parsley
Dry white wine
Red wine vinegar
Boiled potatoes tossed in
    parsley (for accompaniment)
Salt, peppercorns
Cooking fat, 30 g; 1 oz; 2 tbsp

Serves: 4	
Preparation: 10'+2h	
Cooking: 10'	
Difficulty: ●	
Flavour: ● ● ●	
Kcal (per serving): 487	
Proteins (per serving): 41	
Fats (per serving): 15	
Nutritional value: ● ● ●	

1 Rinse the liver and cut it into thin, rectangular slices. Marinate these for 2 hours in a bowl with a glass of wine, a drop of vinegar, the peeled and finely sliced garlic, a bay leaf and 3-4 crushed peppercorns. Turn the slices over every now and then.

2 Remove the slices from the marinade, drain, then briefly fry (one minute each side) in the melted cooking fat (do not let it 'smoke') in a pan. Add the marinade liquid, lower the heat under the pan, season with salt, then cook for 5-6 minutes at the most (otherwise the liver will become tough). Serve sprinkled with chopped parsley and boiled potatoes tossed in parsley.

CARNE EM VINHA-D'ALHOS COM MILHO FRITO

Pork with fried 'polenta' ☛ *Madeira*

Lean pork, 700 g; 1 ¹/₂ lb
1 onion
2 cloves of garlic
Coriander seeds
Ground pimiento
(see Explanations)
Dry white wine
Salt and pepper
Olive oil
For the milho:
Maize flour, 500 g; 1 lb 2 oz;
4 cups
Cooking fat, 10 g; ¹/₂ oz;
¹/₂ tbsp
Salt

Serves:	4
Preparation:	20'-5h
Cooking:	1h 30'
Difficulty:	● ●
Flavour:	● ● ●
Kcal (per serving):	1040
Proteins (per serving):	46
Fats (per serving):	50
Nutritional value:	● ● ●

1 Cut the meat into small chunks and put them in a bowl with the peeled and crushed garlic, about 10 coriander seeds crushed in a mortar, 2 glasses of wine, and a pinch each of salt and pepper; cover the bowl and marinate the meat for 4-5 hours, turning it over now and then.

2 Put the maize flour into a bowl and soak it with a little cold water but do not dissolve it. Pour one and a half litres of water (2¹/₂ pints) into a pot (preferably galvanised copper) and melt the cooking fat in it with a pinch of salt; when the water starts to boil, very gradually sprinkle the maize flour into it and cook the *polenta* over intense heat, stirring it continuously with a flat, wooden spoon. Never stop stirring, even when the *polenta* has absorbed all the liquid and has become a thick, stiff mass (if it becomes too dry, or tends to brown, add a few drops of hot water). The *milho* (or *polenta* as it is known in Italy, and even elsewhere now) will take about 45 minutes to cook this way. When it is ready, pour it on to a hard surface (preferably marble) and smooth it out to about 2 cm (one inch) thick to let it cool.

3 Remove the pieces of pork from the marinade and drain them well, keeping the marinade liquid; slowly brown them in a large casserole (preferably earthenware, with a lid) in a couple of tablespoons of oil. When they are browned all over, remove them from the casserole for the time being.

4 Add a further two tablespoons of oil to that left in the casserole and slowly sauté the peeled and finely sliced onion it; when the onion starts to brown, add a teaspoon of ground pimiento and stir to blend the flavours. Then put the pork back in the casserole.

5 Add the marinade liquid; when this starts to boil, taste for salt, cover the casserole and simmer for about 20 minutes. Take the lid off and reduce the sauce. The meat should be very tender at this point; keep warm until it is time to serve it.

6 Cut the *milho* into rectangles about 5 cm long (2¼ inches) and fry them in a pan with 3-4 tablespoons of oil; remove them one by one as soon as they are ready, leave to drain on kitchen paper, sprinkling them with a little salt. Put the pork on a serving platter and serve surrounded by the fried *milho*.

3

4

5

6

COZIDO À PORTUGUESA

Mixed boiled meat with vegetables ☛ *Trás-os-Montes*

Risotto rice, 500 g; 1 lb 2 oz;
  2 1/2 cups
Half a boiling hen (ready for
  use), approx. 750 g; 1 lb 8 oz
Pork spare-ribs, 500 g; 1 lb 2 oz
Half a pig's head
  (with ears and snout)
1 *chouriço*, 1 *chouriço*
  de sangue and 1 *salpicão*
  (see Explanations)
A couple of pieces of beef shin
  bone (preferably with
  marrow; see bottom right)
1 onion
2 cloves of garlic
1 white cabbage
3-4 swede turnips
5-6 potatoes, 5 carrots
8 *rabas* (see bottom right)
Salt and pepper
Olive oil

Serves: 8-10	
Preparation: 30'	
Cooking: 3h 30'	
Difficulty:	● ● ●
Flavour:	● ●
Kcal (per serving):	1178
Proteins (per serving):	67
Fats (per serving):	55
Nutritional value:	● ● ●

Pierce the *chouriço* and the *chouriço de sangue* all over with a toothpick; put them in a casserole with 1.5 litres (2½ pints) of unsalted, cold water, bring to the boil, cook, and then remove from the pan. Pour the cooking liquid into another casserole, adding another 1.5 litres (2½ pints) of cold water and a pinch of salt; add the well-rinsed bones, then bring to the boil, cover the casserole and simmer slowly for about one hour. Add the spare-ribs, the hen, the pig's head and the *salpicão*. Remove the different meats as soon as they are cooked and keep them in a warm place with a couple of ladles of their broth, leaving the rest of it in the casserole. In fact, the trimmed and rinsed vegetables (all except the garlic and onion) are to be cooked in this broth; remove them from the casserole when they are still *al dente*, keep in a warm place and, once more, do not discard the broth but keep it warm. Heat the oven to 100°C (275°F). Using a third casserole (preferably earthenware and suitable for oven cooking), sauté the peeled and chopped onion and the peeled, crushed garlic in 3-4 tablespoons of oil. As soon as the garlic starts to colour, remove it and add the rice, stirring over high heat to 'toast' evenly until it is almost transparent. Add the meat and vegetable broth (dilute with hot water if insufficient – it should be double the volume of the rice). Keep back a little broth for re-heating the meat. Season with salt and pepper and bring to the boil; transfer to the oven and leave there until the rice has absorbed the liquid. Cut the meats into pieces and re-heat in the broth kept for this purpose; arrange on a platter surrounded by the vegetables except the carrots, which must be sliced and served with the cured meats over the rice.

The bone marrow of adult cattle is not at all dangerous for our health, whereas spinal marrow is. However, since shin bones (including those containing marrow) are difficult to find due to the fact that wary customers have caused a down-trend in demand, knee bones (or pig trotters and knuckles) may be used quite safely instead, and will give the broth the right consistency required. Rabas are roots that grow in the Trás-os-Montes region; similar to carrots in shape but thicker and whitish-yellow, their flavour is between a turnip and a carrot. If you cannot find rabas, we suggest you use celeriac, mooli (Indian white radish), daikon (the Chinese version), or bird-rape.

LOMBO DE PORCO COM AMÊIJOAS

Pork with clams ☛ *Alentejo*

Boned loin of pork, 700 g;
   1 ¹/₂ lb
Large clams (ready for use),
   500 g; 1 lb 2 oz
One and a half onions
5 cloves of garlic
1 carrot
1 sweet pepper
4 ripe cooking tomatoes
Bay, fresh coriander and thyme
1 *piri-piri* (see Explanations)
Ground pimiento
   (see Explanations)
1 lemon (for garnish)
Dry white wine
Salt and pepper
Olive oil

Serves:	4
Preparation:	25'+6h
Cooking:	1h
Difficulty:	● ●
Flavour:	● ● ●
Kcal (per serving):	473
Proteins (per serving):	40
Fats (per serving):	22
Nutritional value:	● ●

Trim and rinse the vegetables according to their use. Cut the meat into cubes and put them in a bowl with 2 peeled and crushed cloves of garlic, a bay leaf, a sprig of thyme, 2 glasses of wine, a teaspoonful of ground pimiento, and a pinch each of salt and pepper. Cover the bowl and marinate for 6 hours. Thereafter, drain the cubes of meat (keep the marinade), brown them in a pan with two tablespoons of oil then remove them from the pan for the time being. Sauté the whole onion (chopped) for 7-8 minutes with one clove of garlic, the sliced carrot, the pepper cut into strips and the *piri-piri* without seeds in the oil left in the pan. Put the meat cubes back in the pan and add the marinade; when this starts to boil, add salt to taste, cover the pan and simmer for about 20 minutes. Chop the half onion and sauté it in another pan with the remaining cloves of garlic and 2-3 tablespoons of oil. Add the tomatoes cut into pieces, stir and allow the flavours to blend for 10 minutes, then add the clams, covering the pan to allow them to open. Place the meat and the vegetables cooked with it on a serving platter, surrounding everything with the drained clams. Mix the clam juice with the meat gravy and bring to the boil; remove from the stove, pour the sauce over the ingredients in the platter, garnish with sprigs of fresh coriander and slices of lemon, and serve.

Boned loin of pork, 600 g;
   1 lb 6 oz
Pig liver, 150 g; 5-6 oz
12 small potatoes
2 cloves of garlic
Bay leaf
Coriander seeds
Bunch of turnip tops (for serving)
1 lemon (for serving)
White *Vinho verde*
Green and black olives
   (for accompaniment)
Salt and pepper
Cooking fat
Olive oil

For the belouras:
Plain white flour, 125 g;
   1/4 lb; 1 cup
Maize flour, 250 g; 9 oz; 2 cups
Rye flour, 125 g; 5 oz; 1 cup
Baker's yeast, 20 g; 1 1/2 oz;
   1 1/2 tbsp
Pig liver, 60 g; 2 1/2 oz
1 clove of garlic
Bay leaf
Parsley
Coriander seeds
Fresh orange rind
Sugar
Salt and pepper
Cooking fat

Serves: 6

Preparation:	35'+2h
Cooking:	1h 30'
Difficulty:	● ● ●
Flavour:	● ●
Kcal (per serving):	1141
Proteins (per serving):	42
Fats (per serving):	44
Nutritional value:	● ● ●

ROJÕES COM BELOURAS

Diced pork with 'milho' dumplings ☛ *Minho*

First of all, make the *belouras*. Pound the liver in a mortar (or food mixer) with a pinch of sugar and a teaspoonful of cooking fat to the consistency of paste. Sift the three types of flour into a bowl and mix with yeast dissolved in a little lukewarm water; add the liver paste, a pinch each of salt and pepper, half a teaspoon of crushed coriander seeds and sufficient water to obtain a smooth dough. Make the dough into a ball and leave to rise for 2 hours. Boil the potatoes; drain and peel while still warm. Trim and rinse the turnip tops then blanch them in slightly salted boiling water. Put both the potatoes and turnip tops to one side. When the dough has risen, knead it for a few minutes then divided it and roll it into cylinders 8 cm long and 2 cm thick; 3 1/2 inches long and 1 inch thick (this is best done with wet hands). Pour 1.5 litres (2 1/2 pints) of cold water into a pot, add a pinch of salt, a sprig of parsley, the garlic, a bay leaf and a piece of orange rind; bring to the boil, let the flavours blend for 3-4 minutes, then drop the dumplings in, removing them with a draining spoon as soon as they come to the surface of the water. Drain on a kitchen towel and keep to one side. Dice the loin of pork, putting the meat in an earthenware casserole with a glass of wine, 4-5 tablespoons of oil, the peeled and crushed garlic, a bay leaf, a teaspoon of coriander seeds and a pinch of salt. Bring to the boil, lower the heat and simmer until all the wine has been absorbed. Remove the pieces of pork, drain and keep to one side. Cut the liver into strips, sprinkle with a little salt and brown in the fat left in the casserole (add more cooking fat whenever necessary); brown the boiled potatoes then, last of all, the *belouras* cut into rounds. Serve the diced pork with the strips of liver, boiled potatoes, green and black olives, roughly chopped turnip tops, slices of *belouras* and wedges of lemon.

This is a slightly modified version of the traditional recipe, which foresees the use of pig blood in the belouras; since not everybody enjoys this, we have substituted it with pig liver.

VEGETABLES AND PULSES

Beans, which come second place after dried codfish on the list of famous Portuguese dishes, bear the crown in this section, together with butter beans and string beans. Nevertheless, there is a vast variety of vegetables to choose from: pumpkin, aubergines, potatoes, peas, and so on. The recipes selected here are mainly for rich side-dishes, with suggestions as to which type of food they match best, but there are also a few recipes that could actually become vegetarian second courses, or at least dishes where vegetables dominate.

5

ABÓBORA E BERINGELAS FRITAS

Deep-fried pumpkin and aubergine ☛ *Beira Baixa*

One piece of yellow pumpkin, 400 g; 12 oz
2 aubergines
1 egg
Plain flour, 50 g; 2 oz; $^1/_2$ cup
Parsley (for garnish)
1 lemon (for garnish)
Fine and course salt
Frying oil

Serves:	4-6
Preparation:	20'+4h
Cooking:	20'
Difficulty:	● ●
Flavour:	● ●
Kcal (per serving):	335
Proteins (per serving):	6
Fats (per serving):	27
Nutritional value:	● ● ●

Peel the pumpkin and cut it into thick slices; put these to soak in slightly salted water for 3-4 hours. Thereafter, drain and dry the pumpkin slices, cutting them this time into thin slices. While the pumpkin is soaking, peel the aubergines, cut them into thick slices, put them in layers on a flat dish (sprinkling each layer with coarse salt) and weigh down with a heavy object for about 30 minutes to let the bitterness 'sweat out'; rinse the slices well, dry, then cut them into strips.

Make a batter (not too thick) with the beaten egg, the flour and a little cold water. Dip the slices of pumpkin and aubergine into it and fry them in plenty of hot oil until golden crisp; remove the vegetables when ready and drain on kitchen paper. Sprinkle with a little table salt and serve decorated with sprigs of parsley and slices of lemon as accompaniment to dried codfish or roast meat dishes.

BATATAS DE CAÇOILA

Stewed potatoes ☞ *Beira Alta*

6 medium-sized, white pulp potatoes	
4 ripe cooking tomatoes	
1 onion	
Salt and pepper	
Olive oil	

Serves: 4	
Preparation: 15′	
Cooking: 35′	
Difficulty: ●●	
Flavour: ●●	
Kcal (per serving): 310	
Proteins (per serving): 7	
Fats (per serving): 11	
Nutritional value: ●●●	

Rinse the potatoes and boil them for 15 minutes; drain and peel while still hot and keep to one side. Peel and roughly chop the onion then gently sauté it (without allowing it to colour) in a casserole (preferably earthenware) with 4-5 tablespoons of oil. Add the rinsed tomatoes (remove the seeds and cut into pieces) and simmer for about ten minutes.

Cut the potatoes into even-sized cubes and add to the casserole; season with salt and pepper and stew slowly until the potatoes start to become mushy. Remove from the heat and serve with grilled second courses.

Small potatoes, 800 g;
 1 3/4 lb
3-4 cloves of garlic
Bay leaf
Ground pimiento
Salt and pepper
Olive oil

Serves: 6	
Preparation: 15'	
Cooking: 30'	
Difficulty: ●●	
Flavour: ●●●	
Kcal (per serving): 311	
Proteins (per serving): 7	
Fats (per serving): 11	
Nutritional value: ●●●	

BATATAS DE REBOLÃO

Pan-roasted potatoes ☛ *Ribatejo*

Rinse the potatoes and boil for 15 minutes; drain and peel while still hot. Pour 6-7 tablespoons of oil into an earthenware pan and slowly sauté the peeled and chopped garlic with a tablespoon of ground pimiento, a bay leaf and a pinch each of salt and pepper.
Add the potatoes (keep them whole) and slowly brown, stirring frequently to allow them to brown all over; taste for salt. When the potatoes are golden-brown, drain them and serve them with fish or roast meat dishes.

CHICHARROS

Cowpeas with vinegar ☞ *Trás-os-Montes*

Leave the cowpeas to soak for 4-5 hours then put them in a pot with plenty of unsalted, cold water; cover the pot, bring slowly to the boil, lower the heat to minimum and simmer for 40 minutes. Before removing the pan from the heat, add a pinch of salt, wait a few minutes, then turn off the heat. Drain the beans (keep the cooking liquid) and keep in a warm place. Trim and rinse the turnip tops. Trim the cabbage, shred it into thin slices and boil with the turnip tops in the water where the cowpeas were cooked. When the cabbage and turnip tops are almost cooked (*al dente*), put the cowpeas back in the pot, stir, then remove from the heat. Drain the vegetables and cowpeas well; put them into a serving dish and dress with oil and vinegar. This is an excellent side dish for second courses made with meat or dried codfish.

Dry cowpeas, 300 g; 12 oz;
  2 1/2 cups
Half a white cabbage
Bunch of turnip tops
Red wine vinegar
Salt
Olive oil

Serves:	4-6
Preparation:	10'+5h
Cooking:	1h
Difficulty:	● ●
Flavour:	● ●
Kcal (per serving):	306
Proteins (per serving):	15
Fats (per serving):	11
Nutritional value:	● ●

ERVILHAS À MODA DO ALGARVE

Peas with poached eggs ☞ *Algarve*

Shelled, fresh peas, 500 g;
  1 lb 2 oz
1 onion
4 eggs
Fresh coriander and parsley
Sugar
Salt and pepper
Olive oil

Serves: 4	
Preparation: 10'	
Cooking: 30'	
Difficulty: ● ● ●	
Flavour: ● ●	
Kcal (per serving): 386	
Proteins (per serving): 20	
Fats (per serving): 20	
Nutritional value: ● ● ●	

Put the peas in a large casserole (preferably earthenware with a lid) together with the peeled onion cut into wedges, the coriander tied into a bunch, a few sprigs of parsley and 5 tablespoons of oil. Stew slowly for 5-6 minutes, stirring all the time. Cover the peas with plenty of water, season with salt and pepper, put the lid on the casserole and bring to the boil; add a pinch of sugar, lower the heat to minimum and simmer for about 25 minutes. About 3-4 minutes before the end of cooking time, break the eggs into the water where the peas are simmering and poach them (use two tablespoons to close the whites around the yolks). Switch off the heat, remove the eggs with a draining spoon, eliminate the bunch of coriander and drain the peas. Serve both peas and poached eggs together, allowing guests to help themselves to salt and pepper. Besides being delicious with fish, this is a fine vegetarian second course that can be completed with servings of cheese.

FAVAS À ALGARVIA

Broad beans with cured meats ☛ *Algarve*

Podded, fresh broad beans,
  400 g; 12 oz; 2 ³/₄ cup
Morcela (see Explanations),
  100 g; 4 oz
Lard (in one piece), 80 g; 3 oz
Mint, parsley
Salt

Serves: 4	
Preparation: 10′	
Cooking: 40′	
Difficulty: ● ●	
Flavour: ● ●	
Kcal (per serving): 315	
Proteins (per serving): 13	
Fats (per serving): 26	
Nutritional value: ● ● ●	

Blanch the broad beans for about 30 minutes in slightly salted boiling water, in a pot with its lid on, together with a sprig each of fresh mint and parsley; drain them while *al dente*. In the meantime, cut the *morcela* into round slices and the lard into tiny cubes; put these in an earthenware casserole (with a lid) with a little water and slowly brown (covered) for about 10 minutes. Put the cooked, broad beans in a tureen, pour the juicy fat from the cured meats over them, mix well then garnish with the cooked meats. This is a rich side dish for fish or white meat, but if served with a salad it can become a delicious second course on its own.

ESPARREGADO DE FEIJÃO VERDE

Golden string beans ☞ *Beira Alta*

Top and tail the string beans and eliminate the filament; rinse well then blanch for 20 minutes in slightly salted boiling water. Drain and cut into pieces 3-4 cm long (1½ - 2 inches). Sauté the peeled garlic in a pan with 5-6 tablespoons of oil; when it colours, remove it and put the beans in its place.

Sift the flour over them, taste for salt and toss-fry over intense heat, stirring well. Pour a drop of vinegar over the beans, allow it to evaporate while still stirring.

Serve the beans, garnished with sprigs of parsley, as an accompaniment to meat dishes.

String (French) beans, 500 g; 1 lb 2 oz
1 clove of garlic
Plain flour, 15 g; ½ oz; 1 tbsp
Red wine vinegar
Fresh parsley (for garnish)
Salt
Olive oil

Serves: 4
Preparation: 15'
Cooking: 30'
Difficulty: ● ●
Flavour: ● ● ●
Kcal (per serving): 126
Proteins (per serving): 3
Fats (per serving): 10
Nutritional value: ● ●

FEIJOADA À PORTUGUESA

Beans with salamis ☞ *Estremadura*

Soak the beans in water 4-5 hours before starting the recipe. Peel the onion and the garlic; rinse the tomatoes and remove their seeds. Drain the beans, put them in a pot and cover them with plenty of cold water; add a tablespoon of oil, a pinch of salt and half an onion speared with the clove. Cover the pot, bring to the boil, lower the flame to minimum and simmer for about 30 minutes. Thereafter, drain the beans (keep the cooking liquid) and keep in a warm place. Make tiny holes in the *chouriço de sangue* and the *farinheira* with a toothpick and cook them in the liquid where the beans have boiled (if this is too thick, dilute it with a little hot water). In the meantime, chop the other half of the onion with the garlic and sauté in a casserole with 3-4 tablespoons of oil; add the tomatoes cut into pieces and allow the flavours to blend for a short while. Add the diced lard, the *chouriço de carne*, a bay leaf and a sprig of parsley; then one or two ladles of the liquid in which the salamis are cooking. As soon as the ingredients start to boil, add the beans, season with salt and pepper then gently simmer for about 15 minutes, until the liquid has reduced. Serve the beans with the salamis cut into rounds. As you can see, this is a rich side dish for six, but it can easily become a full second course for four.

Dry haricot beans, 350 g; 12 oz; 2 ¹/2 cups
Lard (in one piece), 50 g; 2 oz
Chouriço de carne (see Explanations), 100 g; 4 oz
Chouriço de sangue (see Explanations), 60 g; 3 oz
Farinheira (see Explanations), 100 g; 4 oz
2 ripe cooking tomatoes
1 onion, 1 clove
2 cloves of garlic
Bay leaf, parsley
Salt and pepper
Olive oil

Serves: 6	
Preparation: 20'+5h	
Cooking: 1h 15'	
Difficulty: ● ●	
Flavour: ● ● ●	
Kcal (per serving): 905	
Proteins (per serving): 55	
Fats (per serving): 52	
Nutritional value: ● ● ●	

FEIJÃO VERDE À ALENTEJANA

Stewed string beans 🖝 *Alentejo*

1

2

A view of Évora, one the most fascinating cities in Portugal.

1 Trim and rinse all the vegetables according to their use, remembering to peel the potatoes and to top and tail the string beans, eliminating their filaments. Finely chop the garlic and onion and slowly sauté in a casserole (preferably earthenware) with 2-3 tablespoons of oil and the cooking fat.

2 Add the bouquet garni, the tomatoes and a drop of hot water. Simmer slowly, mashing the tomatoes with the back of a wooden spoon.

3 Add the sliced carrot and simmer again for a few minutes, then add the string beans (sliced in two with a diagonal cut), the diced potatoes and a little hot water. Season with salt and pepper and continue to simmer, adding more hot water every now and then as the liquid is absorbed, until the vegetables are cooked but not too soft (*al dente*).

4 In the meantime, cut the bread into thin slices and arrange these in a large tureen; when the vegetables are ready remove the bouquet garni and pour them over the bread. Let the ingredients stand for a few minutes before serving. This is a delicious accompaniment to hearty dishes made with salamis or red meat, but if sprinkled generously with grated cheese, it can also be a nutritious bread soup.

		Serves: 6-8
String (French) beans, 700 g; 1 ¹/₂ lb	Bouquet garni, tied (bay leaf and parsley)	Preparation: 20'
4 ripe cooking tomatoes	Salt and pepper	Cooking: 30'
3 potatoes	Cooking fat, 10 g; ¹/₃ oz; ³/₄ tbsp	Difficulty: ● ●
1 carrot	Olive oil	Flavour: ● ●
1 onion		Kcal (per serving): 406
1 clove of garlic		Proteins (per serving): 11
Stale farmhouse bread, 200 g; 8 oz		Fats (per serving): 13
		Nutritional value: ● ● ●

TOMATADA COM BATATAS

Potatoes with tomato sauce ☞ *Alto Douro*

8 ripe cooking tomatoes
5 medium-sized, white pulp
  potatoes
1 sweet pepper
1 onion
Salt
Jamaica peppercorns
  (see page 61)
Olive oil

Serves:	6
Preparation:	20'
Cooking:	40'
Difficulty:	●●
Flavour:	●●●
Kcal (per serving):	297
Proteins (per serving):	7
Fats (per serving):	11
Nutritional value:	●●

1 Trim and prepare the vegetables according to their use. Finely chop the onion and sauté it in a casserole (preferably earthenware) with 4-5 tablespoons of oil. Add the sweet pepper, sliced crosswise into rings, and simmer until it is tender.

2 Add the tomatoes cut into pieces, stew slowly, mashing the pulp as soon as it becomes soft; season with salt and 7-8 Jamaica peppercorns. Simmer gently without a lid so that the sauce reduces. In the meantime, boil the potatoes in slightly salted water and peel them while still hot. Serve the *tomatada* with the potatoes sliced into rounds as accompaniment to dishes made with locally caught fish, dried codfish or white meat.

Cakes and Desserts

Dulcis in fundo – *a really appropriate statement here! While Portuguese cooking, taken as a whole, can be considered one of the foremost in the world, it distinguishes itself in the art of confectionery and baking: hundreds of years of Lusitanian civilisation are condensed in its unparalleled range of cakes and sweets, delicacies that sumptuously represent the extraordinary, generous nature of this country. Seeing and tasting such masterpieces of love and patience as the Fios-de-ovos, or Charcada and other tempting sweetmeats, we can almost see them being made by the lily-white hands of the nuns who used to make them in their convents for feast-days or for their everyday meals. This tradition is common to the ecclesiastic spheres of many Latin lands, including Sicily; fortunately, in a combination of sacred and worldly, it continues to hand us down heavenly, mouth-watering delicacies such as* Broinhas de Natal, Folar da Páscoa, *the famous* Tigelada *and the celebrated* Toucinho do céu.

6

ALETRIA COM OVOS

Sweet spaghetti ☞ *Douro*

Fine or thin ribbon spaghetti,
  150 g; 6 oz
Castor sugar, 180 g; 6-8 oz;
  1 ¹/₄ cups
4 egg yolks, cinnamon powder
Full milk, half a litre; ³/₄ pint
Rind of one lemon
Butter, 40 g; 1 ¹/₂ oz; 4 tbsp

Serves:	4
Preparation:	10'
Cooking:	20'
Difficulty:	● ●
Kcal (per serving):	574
Proteins (per serving):	19
Fats (per serving):	22
Nutritional value:	● ● ●

1 Cook the spaghetti in boiling water (unsalted, obviously, since this is a dessert) for 3 minutes then drain. Pour the milk into a casserole, add the sugar and the finely grated lemon rind; when it starts to boil, add the spaghetti and cook until not too soft (*al dente*).

2 Add the butter and remove the casserole from the stove, stirring with care. Blend in the beaten egg yolks and put the casserole back on the stove for a few seconds until the sauce thickens. Serve the spaghetti on a platter and make designs on the top with cinnamon powder.

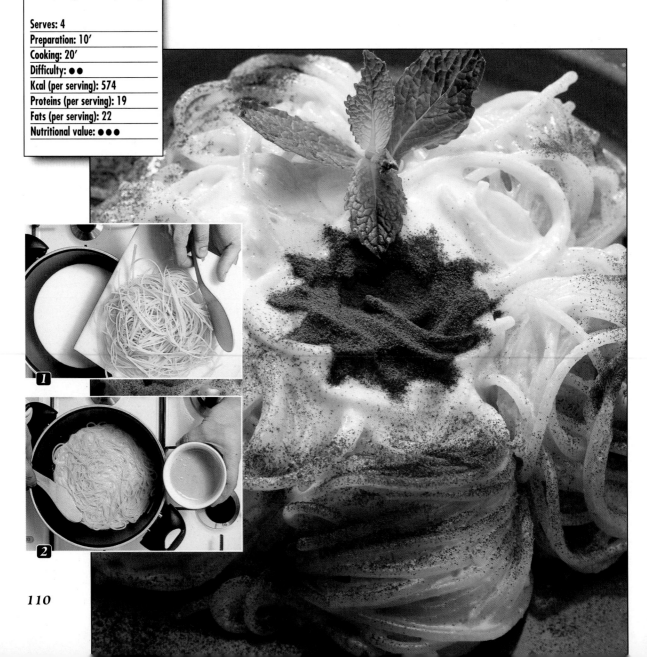

ARROZ DOCE

Sweetened rice ☞ *Minho*

Baking rice, 250 g; 9 oz;
 1 ^{1}/2 cups
Full milk, ^{3}/4 litre; 1 ^{1}/3 pints
Castor sugar, 220 g; 9 oz;
 2 ^{1}/4 cups
3 egg yolks
Rind of one lemon
Salt, cinnamon powder

Serves: 4	
Preparation: 15'	
Cooking: 25'	
Difficulty: ● ●	
Kcal (per serving): 612	
Proteins (per serving): 18	
Fats (per serving): 13	
Nutritional value: ● ● ●	

Pour the milk into a casserole, add the sugar and slowly bring to the boil; add the rice, the finely grated lemon rind, mix carefully, then cook over low heat until the rice is ready.
Remove the casserole from the heat and blend in the egg yolks beaten with a pinch of salt. Mix and put the casserole once more on the stove to allow all the flavours to blend. Turn out the sweetened rice onto a platter, sprinkle with powdered cinnamon and serve.

BROINHAS DE NATAL

Christmas buns ☛ *Beira Litoral*

Yellow pumpkin, 800 g; 1 3/4 lb	
Plain flour, 500 g; 1 lb 2 oz; 4 cups	
Maize flour, 150 g; 6 oz;1 1/4 cups	
Castor sugar, 150 g; 6 oz; 1 1/4 cups	
Sultanas, 80 g; 3 oz; 3/4 cup	
Shelled walnuts, 80 g; 3 oz; 3/4 cup	
Pine nuts, 50 g; 2 1/2 oz; 1/2 cup	
Cinnamon powder, aniseeds	
Baker's yeast, 20 g; 2/3 oz	
Salt	
Butter, 30 g; 1 oz; 2 tbsp	

Serves: 8-10	
Preparation: 35'+3h	
Cooking: 35'	
Difficulty: ●●	
Kcal (per serving): 524	
Proteins (per serving): 12	
Fats (per serving): 12	
Nutritional value: ●●●	

1 Soak the sultanas in lukewarm water. Peel the pumpkin, blanch it in salted, boiling water for 10 minutes, drain (keep the water), then cut it into pieces, eliminating any seeds or fibrous parts. Put it in a food processor at low speed to obtain a smooth, pliable paste. Sift both types of flour into a large bowl and add the pumpkin paste.

2 Dilute the yeast in a little lukewarm water and add it to the mixture in the bowl; blend with a hand mixer, adding sufficient pumpkin water to obtain a stiff, smooth dough.

3 Add the sugar and a pinch each of aniseed and cinnamon, continuing to work the dough gently until it becomes a compact mass in which bubbles start to form. Cover the bowl with a clean kitchen cloth and leave to rise for 3 hours.

4 Squeeze the water out of the sultanas and add them to the dough, together with the pine nuts and the finely chopped walnut kernels. Divide the dough into balls big enough to make round buns (about 8 cm diameter and 2 cm thick; 3 1/2 x 1 inch). Place them on an oven tray greased with butter and bake in the oven preheated to 220°C (410°F) for 20-25 minutes, until cooked inside and golden brown on the outside.

BOLO-PODRE

Honey cake ☛ *Alentejo*

6 eggs
Plain flour, 350 g; 12 oz; 3 cups
Honey, 350 g; 12 oz; 1 1/2 cups
Castor sugar, 250 g; 10 oz;
   2 cups
Baker's yeast, 15 g; 1/2 oz
Rind of one lemon
Cinnamon powder
Olive oil

Serves: 8	
Preparation: 25'+1h	
Cooking: 40'	
Difficulty: ● ●	
Kcal (per serving): 725	
Proteins (per serving): 12	
Fats (per serving): 32	
Nutritional value: ● ● ●	

1 Pour 2 dl (8 fl oz) of oil into a bowl. Add the honey and the sugar; mix with a hand mixer on low speed to obtain a light, creamy consistency, then add the finely grated lemon rind and a teaspoon of cinnamon powder.

2 Blend in the yolks of the eggs one by one, leaving the mixture to stand a few minutes between one addition and another. In the meantime, whisk the egg whites to stiff peaks. Using a hand mixer, add the flour to the honey mixture, then the yeast diluted in a little lukewarm water and lastly, very gently, fold in the whisked egg whites. Cover the mixture with a clean cloth and leave to stand for about one hour. Thereafter, turn it out into a well-oiled cake tin (with removable sides), smooth the surface, cover it with oiled, greaseproof paper and bake in the oven preheated to 200°C (375-400°F) for about 20 minutes. Remove the paper from the top of the tin then put it back into the oven to finish baking (about another 15 minutes). When baked golden-brown, remove from the oven, allow it to cool a few minutes then turn it out onto a plate and serve.

CAVACAS DAS CALDAS DA RAINHA

Sugar-glazed cookies ☛ *Estremadura*

1 This recipe requires little fluted cookie tins, approximately 8 cm diameter and 1 cm deep (3 ½ x ½ inches). Break the eggs into a bowl, sift the flour over them and blend with a hand mixer; add the softened butter and blend until the mixture is of a smooth, pliable consistency; make it into a ball and allow to stand for a few minutes. Divide the mixture among the oiled cookie tins, smooth the surfaces and bake in the oven preheated to 200°C (375- 400°F) for 30 minutes. Remove from the oven but wait until the cookies are cold before turning them out of their tins.

2 Melt the sugar with a drop of water in the top bowl of a double-boiler (with boiling water underneath for *bain-marie* cooking), stirring gently and continuously until the syrup is transparent. Remove from the heat and whip it delicately with a hand whisk until it becomes opaque and thick. Using kitchen prongs or a pair of forks, dip the cookies one after the other in the glaze, coating them well. Leave them to dry (not overlapping) on a cake rack.

4 eggs
Plain flour, 200 g; 8 oz; 1 ¼ cups
Castor sugar, 250 g; 10 oz; 1 ⅓ cups
Butter, 30 g; 1 oz; 2 tbsp
Olive oil

Serves: 4	
Preparation: 15'	
Cooking: 25'	
Difficulty: ● ●	
Kcal (per serving): 793	
Proteins (per serving): 15	
Fats (per serving): 42	
Nutritional value: ● ● ●	

CHARCADA

Crown of caramel egg ribbons ☛ *Beira Litoral*

6 whole eggs + 3 yolks	
Castor sugar, 500 g; 1 lb 2 oz;	
4 cups	
Multi-coloured 'hundreds and	
thousands' (confectioner's	
decoration)	

Serves:	6
Preparation:	15'
Cooking:	20'
Difficulty:	● ● ●
Kcal (per serving):	481
Proteins (per serving):	16
Fats (per serving):	14
Nutritional value:	● ● ●

1 Break the eggs into a bowl, add the yolks and stir with a spoon (do not whisk) until blended. Put 350 g (14 oz; 2 3/4 cups) of sugar and a full glass of cold water into a large pot and heat slowly until dissolved (do not allow to boil). With the heat at minimum, whip the syrup delicately with a hand whisk until it thickens. At this point, using the same method as that described for the *Fios-de-ovos* (page 118) drop the egg mixture over the syrup with circular movements; the egg 'ribbons' will cook immediately.

2 When all the egg mixture has been used up, coat the ribbons with the syrup: using a wooden spatula, scoop up syrup from the centre of the pot and gently fold it in at the sides, turning the ribbons over carefully and stirring to avoid them sticking to the pot. When the ribbons start to dry, and toast brown in colour, remove the pot from the heat. Shape the ribbons into a 'crown' on a cake dish (preferably made of glass). Put the remaining sugar in a small pot with a drop of water; caramelise into a thin toffee and drizzle it over the *charcada*, sprinkling 'hundreds and thousands' over the top to decorate.

FIGOS RECHEADOS

Stuffed figs ☞ *Algarve*

1 Blanch the almonds in unsalted, boiling water; drain, peel and finely grind in a food processor (the result must not be a paste but rather a fine granulate). Transfer this to a bowl, add the sugar, cocoa, a pinch of cinnamon and the finely grated rind of the lemon, then mix.

2 Remove any stalks left on the dried figs and holding them at both ends pull them to stretch them. Slit them open lengthwise, but do not cut right through, and fill them with the stuffing previously prepared.

Close them with a toothpick and place them side by side on an oven tray. Bake at 160°C (320°F) for about 30 minutes. Remove them from the oven and arrange them on a platter.

The traditional method foresees wrapping the prepared figs in tissue paper so that they resemble cloves of garlic, then they are tied in bunches to look like heads of garlic.

36 dried figs
Shelled almonds, 300 g; 12 oz
Castor sugar, 120 g; 4 ^{1}/4 oz;
   8 tbsp
Cocoa powder, 30 g; 1 oz; ^{1}/4 cup
Cinnamon powder
Rind of one lemon

Serves:	6
Preparation:	30'
Cooking:	40'
Difficulty:	●
Kcal (per serving):	596
Proteins (per serving):	16
Fats (per serving):	30
Nutritional value:	● ● ●

FIOS-DE-OVOS

Caramel egg ribbons ☞ *Ribatejo*

2 whole eggs + 10 yolks
   (plus a teaspoon of yolk,
   see Step 2)
Castor sugar, 750 g; 1 lb 12 oz;
   5 cups

Serves:	6-8
Preparation:	20'
Cooking:	20'
Difficulty:	● ● ●
Kcal (per serving):	642
Proteins (per serving):	21
Fats (per serving):	19
Nutritional value:	● ● ●

1 Gently work the whole eggs and yolks in a bowl (do not whip), pass them through a fine sieve several times then leave to stand. Pour a glass of cold water (about 2.5 dl; 10 fl oz) in a wide casserole (you'll soon find out why it has to be wide) and add the sugar; stir over minimum heat until the centre shows signs of beginning to boil. The temperature reached (about 100°C; 212°F) must be kept constant and the syrup should not be allowed to get too thick (in fact, to avoid this when performing the next step it is better to sprinkle the syrup with a teaspoon of egg yolk dissolved in cold water every now and then with your free hand).

2 Fill the appropriate device, or an icing bag (*sac-à-poche*) fixed with a 3 or 4-hole (fine) piping nozzle, with the egg mixture, and holding it as high as possible over the casserole squeeze the mixture as quickly as possible into the hot syrup with circular movements. Balls of thin ribbons will form and will look rather like loose balls of knitting yarn. Remove these balls with a draining spoon and place them over an upturned colander. Wet your hands with cold water and loosen the balls further; dip them in 2-3 tablespoons of the syrup diluted with a little cold water. These *Fios-de-ovos*, also known as *Ovos reais*, are both delicious and decorative, and they are often used in the preparation of other desserts, like *Charcada* (see page 116) or *Lampreia de ovos* (see page 118).

Plain flour, 500 g; 1 lb 2 oz; 4 cups
8 whole eggs + 1 yolk
Full milk, 3 dl; 12 fl oz
Baker's yeast, 20 g; $^3/_4$ oz
Castor sugar, 30 g; 1 oz; 2 tbsp
Aniseed (seeds) and cinnamon powder
Salt
Butter, 100 g; 4 oz; $^1/_2$ cup
Olive oil

Serves:	6
Preparation:	30'+4h
Cooking:	30'
Difficulty:	● ●
Kcal (per serving):	769
Proteins (per serving):	25
Fats (per serving):	41
Nutritional value:	● ● ●

FOLAR DA PÁSCOA

Easter loaf ☞ *Estremadura*

1 Sift one-fifth (100 g; 4 oz; $^1/_2$ cup) of the flour into a bowl, add the yeast diluted in a little lukewarm water and a level tablespoonful of sugar; mix with a hand mixer. Shape the dough obtained into a small loaf, wrap in a clean cloth and leave to rise for one hour. In another, bigger bowl, work the remaining flour with 2 eggs, the remaining sugar and the milk to obtain a smooth, light dough. Add the softened butter, a teaspoonful of crushed aniseed, one of cinnamon, and a pinch of salt. Mix all the ingredients then incorporate, very gently, the first dough when it has risen; cover with the cloth and leave to rise for 3 hours.

2 In the meantime, boil the eggs for 5 minutes (from the first boil), remove them from the water but do not shell them. Divide the risen dough into two unequal parts ($^2/_3$ and $^1/_3$): flatten out the larger piece into a thick round and place on an oiled oven tray; arrange the eggs (in their shells) over the dough and gently press them down until they are half submerged; cover with thick, wide strips made from the remaining dough. Brush all over with beaten egg and bake in a preheated oven (220°C; 410-450°F), for 30 minutes. As its name suggests, this is the traditional Easter bread.

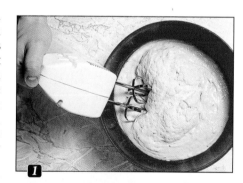

LAMPREIA DE OVOS

Fake 'lamprey-eel' ☞ *Beira Litoral*

1 Put the egg yolks in a bowl and mix them but do not whip them; pass them through a fine sieve several times then leave them to stand. Pour a full glass of cold water into a wide casserole and add the sugar; stirring all the time, dissolve the sugar very slowly until the centre shows signs of beginning to boil. Keep the temperature of the syrup constant (the best way of doing this is to use a double-boiler).

2 Drop spoonfuls of the filtered egg yolks into the syrup: these will 'set' into a sort of dough; remove them one after the other with a draining spoon as soon as they are ready and keep in a warm place.

3 Blanch, peel and grind the almonds; add them to the syrup left in the casserole after Step 2, bring to the boil again, remove from the heat and fold in the 6 mixed but not beaten eggs; put back on the stove until it has thickened a little.

4 Using about ¾ of the cooked egg (Step 2), mould it into the shape of an open ring, with one of the ends thinner and pointed (just like the tail of a lamprey-eel, in fact!); place it on a round cake plate (preferable made of glass). Cover the ring with the egg and almond mixture, smoothing the surface, eliminating any lumps and wiping off any drops that have fallen onto the borders of the plate. Lastly, completely cover the 'eel' with the rest of the cooked egg, smoothing it over the surface. Use chocolate drops to make the lamprey's eyes and gently score the surface of the 'eel' with a sharp knife to fake the scales. Arrange *Fios-de-ovos* (follow recipe on page 118) all around the plate and serve at room temperature.

6 whole eggs + 18 yolks
Castor sugar, 500 g; 1 lb 2 oz; 4 cups
Shelled almonds, 100 g; 4 oz; 4 tbsp
Fios-de-ovos (see page 118): prepare beforehand, using the proportions for 1 whole egg and 5 yolks
Chocolate drops (for decoration)

Serves:	8
Preparation:	35'
Cooking:	35'
Difficulty:	● ● ●
Kcal (per serving):	2117
Proteins (per serving):	157
Fats (per serving):	119
Nutritional value:	● ● ●

PÃO-DE-LÓ DE AMÊNDOAS

Almond cake ☞ *Alentejo*

7 eggs
Shelled almonds, 250 g; 9 oz;
  3 ¹/₂ tbsp
Castor sugar, 250 g; 9 oz;
  2 cups
Plain flour, 80 g; 3 oz; ¹/₂ cup
  (plus extra for flouring the
  cake tin)
Icing (see Step 4) or whipped
  cream (for decorating)
Candied orange peel
  (for decorating)
Butter, 20 g; ³/₄ oz; 1 ¹/₂ tbsp

Serves: 6	
Preparation: 20'	
Cooking: 1h 10'	
Difficulty: ● ●	
Kcal (per serving): 977	
Proteins (per serving): 26	
Fats (per serving): 57	
Nutritional value: ● ● ●	

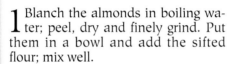

1 Blanch the almonds in boiling water; peel, dry and finely grind. Put them in a bowl and add the sifted flour; mix well.

2 Separate the egg whites from the yolks. Put the yolks in a second bowl, add the sugar and beat with a hand mixer until the mixture is creamy and fluffy.

3 Whip the egg whites, with a pinch of salt, to stiff peaks in another bowl; add very gently to the beaten yolks, folding in the flour and almond mixture.

4 Pour the mixture obtained into a cake tin (with removable sides) greased with butter and dusted with flour; smooth the surface of the cake and put in the oven preheated to 200°C (375-400°F); lower the heat to 140°C (300°F) immediately. Bake until ready (about one hour), then turn the cake out on to a serving plate. Decorate the top of the cake when cool with icing (made with icing sugar, a drop of milk and lemon or orange juice), or whipped cream, and a border of candied orange peel.

A spectacular sunset enhances the church in Mértola, near Beja.

PASTEÍS DE NATA

Custard-cream pastries ☛ *Estremadura*

1

2

For the pastry:
Plain flour, 250 g; 9 oz; 2 cups
(plus extra for flouring the pastry board)
Butter, 210 g; 8 oz; 1 cup

For the filling:
Fresh cream, 2.5 dl; 8 fl oz
4 egg yolks
Plain flour, 15 g; ¹/₂ oz; 1 tbsp
Castor sugar, 100 g; 4 oz;
    ³/₄ cup
Finely grated rind of one lemon
Icing sugar (for decorating)

Serves:	6
Preparation:	35'÷30'
Cooking:	30'
Difficulty:	● ●
Kcal (per serving):	763
Proteins (per serving):	13
Fats (per serving):	52
Nutritional value:	● ● ●

1 This recipe requires little cake tins measuring approximately 8-10 cm (3¹/₂-4 inches) in diameter and 1 cm (half an inch) deep. Make the pastry: sift the flour into a bowl, mix (using a hand mixer) with sufficient lukewarm water to obtain a soft, smooth dough; leave to stand for 15 minutes. In the meantime, soften the butter by squashing it with the back of a fork. Briefly knead the dough by hand then shape it into a block. Roll the block out to obtain a sheet 1 cm (half an inch) thick; spread one third of the softened butter over it (leaving a free border of about 2 cm; one inch), fold the sheet over in three, knead once more by hand then shape it into a block again. Roll the dough out yet again and spread another third of the butter over it, fold as before, knead, then give it its block shape again. Repeat these steps, using up the last third of the butter; let the block stand this time for 15 minutes.

2 Roll the dough out to 3-4 mm thick (¹/₃ inch); cut it into 10-12 cm (4-5 inch) wide strips then roll these up, one by one, into tight cylinders. Cut the cylinders into 1 cm (¹/₂ inch) thick slices; put one 'spiral' of pastry in every cake tin and, using wet thumbs, fit the pastry over the bottom and sides of the tins to line them (do not allow the pastry to go over the rims). To make the filling, mix all the ingredients in a pot, heat over low temperature and bring to the boil mixing gently all the time. As soon as the custard starts to boil, remove immediately from the heat and allow it to cool to lukewarm before pouring it into the individual tins. Smooth the surface of the custard, then bake in the oven preheated to 220°C (410-450°F) until golden brown on top. Remove the pastries from the oven, allow them to cool in their tins, then lift them out. Serve the *pastéis* dusted with icing sugar.

QUEIJADAS DE COIMBRA

Cheese tartlets ☞ *Beira Litoral*

1 This recipe requires small individual, fluted flan tins (approx. 8-10 cm diameter and 1 cm deep; 3¹/₂-4 inches x ¹/₂ inch). Melt the butter very, very slowly in a small pot (preferably a double-boiler for *bain-marie* cooking) – do not allow it to 'smoke' or foam; leave to cool a few minutes. Pour the melted butter into a bowl, add the flour sifted with a pinch of salt, then mix with a hand mixer, adding sufficient lukewarm water to obtain a smooth, soft dough; leave to stand for 30 minutes. In the meantime, prepare the filling in another bowl: blend together (with a hand mixer) the cheese, the egg yolks and the sugar, mixing until the sugar has completely dissolved.

2 Roll out the pastry to a sheet about 4 mm (¹/₃ inch) thick and use this, divided accordingly, to line the tins. Fill the pastry cases with the cheese mixture, smooth the surfaces, put the tins on an oven tray and bake in the oven preheated to 200°C (375-400°F) for about 35 minutes. Switch off the oven and leave the tartlets to cool in the closed oven for 15 minutes. Lift them out of the tins and serve at room temperature.

Unsalted, soft cheese
  (crème fraîche or
  ricotta-cheese), 350 g; 14 oz
Plain flour, 250 g; 10 oz; 2 cups
Castor sugar, 250 g; 10 oz;
  2 cups
6 egg yolks
Salt
Butter, 40 g; 1 ¹/₂ oz; 4 tbsp

Serves:	6
Preparation:	30'+30'
Cooking:	35'+15'
Difficulty:	● ●
Kcal (per serving):	553
Proteins (per serving):	24
Fats (per serving):	19
Nutritional value:	● ● ●

TIGELADA

Baked custard ☞ *Beira Baixa*

Full milk, half a litre; ³/₄ pint
4 eggs
Plain flour, 10 g; ¹/₂ oz;1 tbsp
Demerara sugar, 250 g; 9 oz;
  2 cups
Honey
Rind of one lemon
Olive oil

Serves: 4	
Preparation: 10'	
Cooking: 20'	
Difficulty: ●	
Kcal (per serving): 532	
Proteins (per serving): 15	
Fats (per serving): 23	
Nutritional value: ● ● ●	

Oil individual ovenproof ramekins (or other small, earthenware dishes) and put them in the oven preheated to 220°C (410-450°F). In the meantime, beat the egg yolks (preferably by hand with an egg whisk) with a teaspoonful of honey, the sugar and the finely grated lemon rind; add the flour (a round tablespoonful) and the milk, blending carefully to make it smooth and to avoid lumps. Pour this custard into the ramekins, doing this as quickly as possible when taking them out of the oven (it would be best to leave them inside while doing this – but we don't want you to be in danger of burning yourselves!); put the ramekins back in the oven until the *tigelada* is cooked (approximately 20 minutes).

TOUCINHO DO CÉU

Egg and almond cake ☞ *Douro e Minho*

Blanch the almonds in unsalted, boiling water; drain, peel then grind (all except a couple which will be needed for decorating the cake); the result should be a fine granulate rather than a paste. Beat the egg yolks with the egg white, but do not whip. Soften the butter and mix it into the flour; keep to one side. Pour the sugar into a pot, melt it slowly with 2 dl (8 fl oz) of water, to obtain a clear syrup (stirring continuously). Add the egg yolks beaten with the white, then the ground almonds; mix with a spatula (still over low heat) and allow the custard to thicken. Remove from the heat when it shows signs of separating from the sides of the pot and sticking to the spatula; pour the custard into an ovenproof mould (preferably fancy), smooth the surface and bake in the oven preheated to 200°C (375-400°F) for 35 minutes. When ready, remove the mould and allow the almond custard to cool for a few minutes, then turn it out on to a round serving plate. When the dessert is completely cold, dust it all over with icing sugar and decorate with sprigs of fresh mint and the almonds kept to one side (cut into slivers). And what do we have? A dessert from Paradise. A real *toucinho do céu*, which means: a piece of Heaven!

12 egg yolks and one white
Castor sugar, 500 g; 1 lb 2 oz; 4 cups
Shelled almonds, 250 g; 9 oz; 2 cups
Cinnamon in powder
Plain flour, 15 g; ^{1}/2 oz; 1 tbsp
Icing sugar (for decoration)
Fresh mint (for decoration)
Butter, 50 g; 1 ^{3}/4 oz; 5 tbsp

Serves: 6	
Preparation: 20'	
Cooking: 1h	
Difficulty: ● ●	
Kcal (per serving): 954	
Proteins (per serving): 33	
Fats (per serving): 51	
Nutritional value: ● ● ●	